WY PLAY HOUSE

Sunbeam Terrace

By **Mark Catley**

Director **Alex Chisholm**
Designer **Emma Williams**
Lighting Designer **Tim Skelly**
Sound Designer **Glen Massam**
ASM **Christine Guthrie**

First performance:
Courtyard Theatre, West Yorkshire Playhouse,
27 March 2003

West Yorkshire Playhouse
Quarry Hill
Leeds
LS2 7UP
www.wyp.org.uk

The Company

Ron Blass Old Man
Mick Martin Hardman
Dorian Smith Teenage Boy
Sally Walsh Lap Dancer
Gary Whitaker Dealer

Lapdancing consultancy
Rachel Anstis at Hot Promotions
and Emma Gibson at DV8

BSL Interpreted performance
Friday 11 April 7.45pm
BSL Interpreter
Alan Haythornthwaite

Audio Described performances
Thursday 10 April 2.30pm
Saturday 12 April 7.45pm
Audio Describers
Jo Davy, Anne Shadbolt and Neil Scott

THERE WILL BE NO INTERVAL FOR THIS PERFORMANCE

Smoking in the auditorium is not permitted. Please ensure that mobile
phones, pagers and digital alarms are switched off before you enter
the auditorium.

Cast

Ron Blass Old Man

Ron has lived in Leeds all his life. He worked as one of the Bevin Boy coalminers during the war and subsequently ran his own pharmacy business for many years. Theatre credits include: *Macbeth* (Pocket Theatre, Tour); *A House by the Sea* (Leeds Actors Company); *A Common Chorus* (Leeds University); *The Cherry Orchard*, *One Flew Over the Cuckoo's Nest* (Leeds Playhouse). Film and television credits include: *Coronation Street*, *Cardiac Arrest*, *Hetty Wainthropp Investigates*, *Fanny and Elvis*. Radio credits include: *Jonathan Martin* for BBC Radio York.

Mick Martin Hardman

Mick Martin lives in Bradford; as a playwright his work includes: *Once upon a Time in Wigan* (Contact Theatre, Manchester and West Yorkshire Playhouse); *The Life and Times of Young Bob Scallion*, (West Yorkshire Playhouse and Northcott Theatre, Exeter); *Stepper Joe's Wicked Beat* (West Yorkshire Playhouse Schools Company); *The Immigrant Song, A Weekend in England*. Television writing credits include series as diverse as *Ballykissangel*, *Dream Team* and even *Crossroads*. This is Mick's first appearance on stage for years and years and should it go well he is considering commissioning a suitable toupee and heading for Hollywood.

Dorian Smith Teenage Boy

Dorian lives in Greengates, Bradford; he has been attending Footsteps Theatre School in Bradford since he was 11 and is currently studying for GCSEs at Immanuel CE Community College. Dorian plays football for his local football team, Ravenscliffe United. Theatre and television credits include being a member of Fagin's gang in the Cameron Mackintosh production of *Oliver!* at the Bradford Alhambra in 1999; *A Night of a Thousand Laughs* with Cannon and Ball at St George's Hall, Bradford; as an extra in CITV's *My Parents are Aliens*, and numerous roles in school and theatre school productions.

Sally Walsh Lap Dancer

Theatre credits include: *Two Tracks & Text Me*, *Shy Gas Man* (West Yorkshire Playhouse); *Cinderella* (The Sands Centre, Carlisle and The Pomegranate, Chesterfield). Film and television credits include: *Real Men*, *City Central*, *Smokescreen* (BBC); *Cold Feet*, *Children's Ward* (Granada); *Fat Friends*, *Heartbeat*, *Emmerdale*, *Tumbledown Farm* (YTV); *Children of Winter* (Central); *The Old Curiosity Shop* (RHI Entertainment). Radio credits include: *Heart Attack*, *Crazy Big Fish*, *The Dinner Ladies* (R4); *The Stonewalkers* (R3).

Gary Whitaker Dealer

This is Gary's third appearance at the West Yorkshire Playhouse. Previously he appeared in *Rita Sue & Bob Too / A State Affair* (Out of Joint) and *Of Mice and Men* (West Yorkshire Playhouse). Other theatre credits include: *Five Kinds of Silence* (Lyric Theatre, Hammersmith); *Lam*, *Bouncers* (Northcott Theatre, Exeter); *Loot* (Chichester Festival and Vaudeville Theatre); *Saturday, Sunday, Monday* (Chichester Festival Theatre); *My Sister in This House* (Theatre Clywd); *Unidentified Human Remains* (Royal Exchange Theatre); *Wildest Dreams* (Royal Shakespeare Company); *The Faerie Queen* (Lisbon Coliseum); *Sally's Suspected*, *Sleeping Ugly*, *Happy Days* (Royal Court Theatre); *Easy Laughter* (Man in the Moon); *One Over the Eight*, *My Very Own Story*, *Wildest Dreams*, *A Man of Letters* (Stephen Joseph Theatre); *The False Servant* (The Gate Theatre); *Brighton Beach Memoirs* (Frankfurt); *Flarepath* (Kings Head Theatre); *The Secret Diary of Adrian Mole* (Wyndhams Theatre); *Master Harold and the Boys* (Jubilee Theatre, Singapore). Film and television credits include: *Holby City*, *In Deep*, *Goggle Eyes*, *The Brittas Empire*, *First of the Summer Wine*, *Pressure*, *Talking in Whispers*, *Have his Carcass* (BBC); *The Vice* (Carlton); *A&E* (Granada); *Sunday* (Channel Four); *Heartbeat* (YTV); *The Bill* (Thames); *The Gathering* (Samuelson Films).

Creatives

Mark Catley Writer

Mark was born in Leeds. He studied Performing Arts at Park Lane College, Leeds and subsequently took a BA in Drama and Theatre Arts at Goldsmith's College, University of London. Writing credits include: *Angel* (City Voice commission 1998, performed by the Theatre Company Blah Blah Blah & Leeds Studio Theatre. Published by Leeds University Press 2003); *Obstacles* – x3 short plays (commissioned by South Leeds Youth Theatre); *Base U.K.* (commissioned and performed by Union City Dance Theatre Company); *Too Broke to Fix* (commissioned and performed by Angel Productions) *Frankie and Johnny* (commissioned and performed by the Theatre Company Blah Blah Blah) and *The Grimp*, a children's book commissioned and performed by Angel Productions.

Alex Chisholm Director

Alex studied History at Oxford University. She spent a year studying with Ian McKellen, Cameron Mackintosh Professor of Contemporary Theatre, before completing the Postgraduate Directing course at Drama Studio London. Alex was appointed Literary Manager at the West Yorkshire Playhouse in December 2001. Previously she spent seven years as a freelance director, assistant director and workshop leader working with companies including Birmingham Rep, Chichester Festival, Royal National Theatre, Red Shift and Paines Plough. In 1997 she set up Convivio Theatre Company. Productions directed included *Pelleas and Melisande* translated by Timberlake Wertenbaker and *A Night with Constantine Cavafy* which she also adapted. In 1995 and 1997 she ran the European Theatre Directors' Forum in Cambridge UK and Athens, Greece respectively, on behalf of the Directors' Guild of Great Britain. She was on the Council of the Directors' Guild from 1995 to 1997.

Emma Williams Designer

Trained at: Wimbledon School of Art. Design work includes: *Visions and Voices* (Unlimited Theatre); *Angel* (Studio Theatre, Leeds); *Small Objects of Desire* (Soho Poly Theatre); *Beauty and the Beast*, *The Magic Finger*, *Ten in a Bed* (Open Hand Theatre Company, UK Tour); *It's a Mad, Mad World My Masters*, *Lords of Creation* (Minerva Studio, Chichester; Elektra (Guildhall Studio). For The Theatre Company Blah Blah Blah: *Stuck*, *Thinskin*, *Unmade Beds*, *One Tribe*, *Grass*, *Antibone* (UK tour); *Frankie and Johnny* (Studio Theatre, Leeds and tour); *Ho! Ho! Ho!* (West Yorkshire Playhouse and tour). As Resident Designer at The Arts Educational School, Chiswick, 1989 – 1992 productions included *The House of Blue Leaves*,

Saturday, Sunday, Monday, *Hedda Gabler*, *The Hypochondriac* and *Aristocrats*. Opera design includes: *La Cenerentola* (Camberwell Pocket Opera); *Admeto*, *Partenope*, *Alceste* (Cambridge Handel Opera Group); *Siroe* (Royal College of Music). TV and Film work includes costume design for BBC Shakespeare series, directed by Fiona Shaw and set decoration for Sands Films' *The Fool*. Emma is a visiting design lecturer at Edge Hill University College Drama Unit, supervising production and teaching model making. She is also works in Leeds schools as a Creative Arts Partnerships in Education (CAPE) artist.

Tim Skelly Lighting Designer

Tim Skelly is a resident theatre designer and academic at the Workshop Theatre, University of Leeds. He has also worked as an academic at University College Bretton Hall in Wakefield and as a resident practitioner and teacher of lighting design at the Royal Academy of Dramatic Art in London. As a freelance lighting designer recent professional credits include: *Union Street* and *Brother Jacques* (Plymouth Theatre Royal); *Romeo and Juliet*, *White Devil*, and *Three Sisters* (Colchester Mercury); *The Coming of Age* (Janet Smith and Dancers tour); *Korczak* (Teatr Muzyczny, Gdynia and Warsaw, Poland); *Ho! Ho! Ho!* (Blah Blah Blah Theatre Co.), *Hijra* and *God's Official* (West Yorkshire Playhouse); *Having a Ball* (York Theatre Royal and Colchester Mercury); *Safety* and *Neutrino*: Fringe First Winner 2001 (Unlimited Theatre); *High Land*, *Daddy I'm Not Well* and *Inside Somewhere* (Scottish Dance Theatre); *Self Observation Without Judgment* and *My House is Melting* (The Peter Darrell Foundation). Tim also works as a lighting consultant for Yorkshire Sculpture Park and has collaborated with several artists, working on lighting designs for Sir Anthony Caro's *The Trojan Wars*, and retrospectives for Philip King and Christo.

Glen Massam Sound Designer

After completing the ABTT Theatre Electricians course Glen became Deputy Chief Electrician at the Fortune Theatre, London and then went on to become Technical Manager of the Theatre Royal, Wakefield, where he stayed for ten years. After five years as Project and Hire Manager for The Music Company, Glen returned to the theatre in 2001 as Chief Sound Technician for the West Yorkshire Playhouse. Throughout his career Glen has undertaken many projects including sound, lighting and event management for hundreds of shows, concerts and other events. Recent sound design credits include: *Carnival Messiah*, *And All The Children Cried*, *Stepping Out* and *Little Shop of Horrors* (West Yorkshire Playhouse).

ARTS FOR ALL AT THE WEST YORKSHIRE PLAYHOUSE

Since opening in 1990, the West Yorkshire Playhouse has established a reputation both nationally and internationally as one of Britain's most exciting and active producing theatres – winning awards for everything from its productions to its customer service. The Playhouse provides both a thriving focal point for the communities of West Yorkshire and theatre of the highest standard for audiences throughout the region and beyond. It produces up to 16 of its own shows each year in its two auditoria and stages over 1000 performances, workshops, readings and community events, watched by over 250,000 people.

Alongside its work on stage the Playhouse has an expansive and groundbreaking programme of education and community initiatives. As well as a busy foyer and restaurant which are home to a range of activities through the week, the Playhouse offers extensive and innovative education programmes for children and adults, a wide range of unique community projects and is engaged in the development of culturally diverse art and artists. It is this 'Arts for All' environment, as well as a high profile portfolio of international theatre, new writing for the stage and major productions with leading artists that has kept the Playhouse constantly in the headlines and at the forefront of the arts scene.

Simon Armitage and **Linda Monaghan** Commis Chefs
Lee Moran, Chris Hill, Callum Stewart and **Lee Dennell** Kitchen Porters
Caron Hawley and **Esther Lewis** Kitchen Assistants
Diana Kendall Restaurant Supervisor
Gail Lambert, Kath Langton and **Gemma Voller** Restaurant Assistants
Sarah Allen, Charlene Kendall, Victoria Burt, Sharisse Ghoneim, Ruth Baxter, Jimmy Dunbar, Emma Harrison and **Jessica Best** Catering Assistants*
Malcolm Salsbury Bar Manager
Sally Thomas and **Jennie Webster** Assistant Bar Managers
Amelia Crouch, Victoria Hemsley, Anna Hill, Marion Miller, Francis Ratcliff, Sophie Pearson, Graeme Thompson and **Tim Varney** Bar Assistants*

Company and Stage Management
Diane Asken Company Manager
Paul Veysey and **Karen Whitting** Stage Managers
Hannah Lobb and **Sarah Northcott** Deputy Stage Managers
Sarah Braybook and **Christine Guthrie** Assistant Stage Managers

Customer Services
Kathy Dean, Jackie Gascoigne and **Rachel Blackeby**

Finance
Teresa Garner Finance Manager
Coleen Anderson Finance Officer
Jenny Copley Cashier
Tatiana Stoyanova Payroll Officer
Fran Major Ledger Clerk

Housekeeping
Doreen Hartley Domestic Services Manager*
Mary Ambrose, Eddy Dube, Harold Hartley, Michaela Singleton, Paul Robinson, Teresa Singleton, Zheng Qi, Sarah Wonnacott and **Dabo Guan** Cleaners*

Maintenance
Frank Monaghan Maintenance Manager
Jim Gaffigan and **Martin McHugh** Maintenance Assistants
Shane Montgomery General Services Assistant

Marketing and Sales
Nick Boaden Marketing Manager
Angela Robertson Sales Manager
Duncan Grant Graphic Design Manager
Sarah Kennedy Senior Marketing Officer
Simon Bedford Marketing Officer
Caroline Gornall Deputy Sales Manager
Lynn Hudson, Mel Worman and **Bronia Daniels** Duty Supervisors
Caroline Dennis, Maureen Kirkby, Sally Thomas, Pene Hayward, Sarah Jennings, Rachael Margrave, Sally Mackay, Lucy Hird, Dena Marsh and **Tom Stoker** Box Office Assistants

New Writing
Alex Chisholm Literary and Events Manager

Paint Shop
Virginia Whiteley Head Scenic Artist
Brian Van Der Heever Freelance Scenic Artist

Performance Staff
Andy Charlesworth and **Jon Murray** Firemen
Rebecca Ashdown, Nathanya Laurent, Jon Dean, Shaun Exley, Simon Howarth, Sally McKay, Hayley Mort, Jo Murray, Soazig Nicholson, Alex Ramseyer, Genevieve Say, Luke Sherman, Jamie Steer, Daneill Whyles, Jemal Cohen, Rachel Blakeby, Fynnwin Prager, Sangeeta Chana, Indy Panesar, Marcus Stewart, Luca Biason, Andrew Ashdown, Simon Biggins, Avril Fredericks, Sophie Goodeve, Deborah Hargreave, Fiona Heseltine, Kimberley Hughes, Sara Lovewell, Monisha Roy, Lewis Smith, Lucy Stenhouse, Holly Thomas, Darrelle Villa, Emily Mann Attendants*
Jessica Kingsley and **Sarah Jennings** Playhouse Hosts*

Press
Rachel Coles Head of Press
Stacey Arnold Press Officer

Production Electricians
Stephen Sinclair Chief Electrician
Julie Rebbeck Deputy Chief Electrician

Christopher Sutherland, Drew
Wallis and Melani Nicola Electricians
Deborah Joyce Temporary
Electricians
Benoit Dupraz Work Placement

Production Management
Suzi Cubbage Production Manager
Eddie de Pledge Production Manager
Christine Alcock Production
Administrator

Props Department
Chris Cully Head of Props
Scott Thompson, Susie Cockram
and Sarah Partridge Prop Makers

Schools Touring Company
Gail McIntyre Director
Ysanne-Marie Morton Touring and
Projects Co-ordinator
Sara Bienvenu, Will Hammond and
John Le Hunte Actors
Marc Walton Technical Assistant

Security
Denis Bray and Darkside Security

Sound Department
Glen Massam Chief Sound Technician
Adrian Parker Deputy Sound
Technician
Martin Pickersgill Sound Technician

Technical Stage Management
Martin Ross Technical Stage Manager
Michael Cassidy Deputy Technical
Stage Manager
Julian Brown Stage Technician

Theatre Operations
Helen Child Head of Operations
Karen Johnson Theatre Manager
Sheila Howarth, Jeni Douglas,
Jonathan Dean Duty Managers*

Wardrobe Department
Stephen Snell Head of Wardrobe
Victoria Marzetti Deputy Head of
Wardrobe
Julie Ashworth Head Cutter
Selina Nightingale Cutter
Alison Barrett Costume Prop Maker/
Dyer
Catherine Lowe and Nicole Martin
Wardrobe Assistants
Anne-Marie Hewitt Costume Hire
Manager
Kim Freeland Wig and Make-up
Supervisor
Catherine Newton Wardrobe
Maintenance / Head Dresser
Joanne Daley, Saran Marsh and Kat
Willis Dresser,

*Denotes part-time
**Internship programme in partnership
with CIDA

West Yorkshire Playhouse Corporate Supporters

Sponsors of the Arts Development Unit

PROVIDENT FINANCIAL

Production Sponsors

Carnival Messiah

The Wizard of Oz

DIRECTORS CLUB

Executive Level Members

O_2

CARLSBERG-TETLEY

EVANS property group

Associate Level Members

parallel
DIGITAL INVENTION

Servicemark
YORKSHIRE • HUMBER

YORKSHIRE POST

Director Level Members

Baker Tilly
Bank of Scotland
British Gas
BWD Rensburg
Crowne Plaza Leeds
David Yablon
GNER
Gordons Cranswick
Grant Thornton
GVA Grimley

Hiscox
New Horizons
Pinsent Curtis Biddle
Provident Financial
True Temper
Thompson Design
Yorkshire Dales Ice Cream
Yorkshire Television

One Performance Sponsors

O_2
Little Shop of Horrors

O_2
Singin' in the Rain

If you would like to learn how your organisation can become involved with the success of the West Yorkshire Playhouse please contact the Corporate Affairs Department on 0113 213 7275 or email networking@wyp.org.uk

First published in 2003 by Oberon Books Ltd.
(incorporating Absolute Classics)
521 Caledonian Road, London N7 9RH
Tel: 020 7607 3637 / Fax: 020 7607 3629

e-mail: oberon.books@btinternet.com
www.oberonbooks.com

A catalogue record for this book is available from the British
Library.

ISBN: 1 84002 369 4

Cover image: Guzelian

Printed in Great Britain by Antony Rowe Ltd, Chippenham.

Characters

DEALER

Twenty-eight, slim build, good-looking, dressed unkempt.
Sells drugs for a living. Is a very changeable character.
Suffers from depression and anxiety. Dropped out of
university but very intelligent. Does not do drugs any more,
but has no morals about selling them.

HARDMAN

Mid- to late-thirties. Very large and imposing. Ex-service
crew (an organised Leeds United hooligan base). Dressed
street-trendy, younger than his age. Is on a personal crusade
to rid the estate of 'scum' (paedophiles, dealers et cetera).
Seems content and happy with his life, but is wracked with
guilt and confusion.

TEENAGE BOY

Fifteen, tall for his age, wiry and full of energy. Dressed
street. Doesn't attend school but is quite smart. Wants to be
a dealer.

OLD MAN

Early eighties. Looks well for it. Was evidently a healthy,
strong man. Dressed simple but smart, needs to keep warm.
Sad eyes but has a warm, likeable character.

LAP DANCER

Early twenties but looks older. Very attractive but slightly
world-weary. Single mum (child one year old). Does too
much speed, which she pays for with private lap-dances. Is
often wired and in a rush. She is convinced that she is 'doing
her best'.

Dedicated to Edith Douglas (truth and honesty)

with thanks to Max Stafford-Clark, Ian Brown, Alex Chisholm, Tom Senior, The Blahs, Jo, Jodie, Big D in OZ and family and friends for all your support x

ACT ONE

DEALER's bedsit. No seats, just a bed. Sink in corner. Tasteful, quite arty, not what would be expected of a drug dealer's decor. HARD MAN, OLD MAN, LAP DANCER and DEALER are in the space.

HARDMAN: Me and me mates, Leeds city centre. Loud, confident and way fucking lairy. (*Sings.*) 'Hooly, hooly, hooligan, hooligan, hooligan, hooly, hooly, hooligan, hooly, hoolY-gannnn!' Ben Sherman shirt, casual kegs, Rockport shoes, not boots, we're not kiddies. People are afraid of me. I'm the one in the middle, staring you out, daring you to look at me. Square on for a square go. And you are fucking shitting it! Don't even think about denying it. And, if the mood takes me, I'll launch you. One hit, lower jaw, teeth on the floor. Just keep your head down and walk past, cos your breath will never taste as sweet as the one you take when I've gone. (*Pause.*) You think you know who I am? You don't know me at all. (*Exits.*)

OLD MAN: I met my first wife when I was seventeen and she was sixteen, we courted for two years then got married, small service, just families. Married for seven years, then I divorced her, same year the Marilyn Monroe film *The Seven Year Itch* came out! Nineteen fifty-five. She never understood the irony of that. Divorce was rare as hen's teeth back then, but I didn't care, my life had been on hold for ten year, long time for a young man. I felt guilty though, God did I. She was a lovely young thing, an innocence about her that would melt your heart and a good wife, in the traditional sense, house clean, food on the table. In seven years of marriage there was never a cross word between us. (*Pause.*) I was bored to tears, not just of her, but of my

15

life. I'd always had a passion for politics and philosophy, ideas above me station as my father would say. This is where the wife couldn't help me. It was too easy with her. I know now that what I needed was an equal, not someone to look after me, I was a grown man. I could take care of myself. (*Laughs, and goes throughout to the next section.*) I was born at the wrong time, I look at the young lassies these days and can't help admiring their spirit, things are different now, harder in a lot of ways, young women don't have defined roles any more, they have to find out who they are. I saw one young girl the other day with a very tight top on, proclaiming THIS BITCH BITES! More power to her, you bite away girl! I was having a sandwich in the café, the other day, sat next to a young couple with a bairn in a pushchair, he says to her 'pass us that'… whatever it was, I can't remember, and she turns round and snaps 'get it yerself you lazy bastard!' Well, I start applauding her, there's a bit of confused silence, wondering what the silly old man's playing at and then everyone's laughing, even the lazy bastard, even the kiddie in the pushchair! I'll always applaud a woman with spirit. Yeah, the women have changed and I approve whole-heartedly. (*Exits.*)

LAP DANCER: I started college last week. Got some childcare sorted out, shouldn't have bothered, place were full of kids anyhow. Tutor at the interview told me they were a lot of mature students doing my course, my eye they were, full of sixteen-year-old scruffs. One oldish fella, cardy and a glass eye, looks like a paedophile, but he won't see the month out. So, me first day there, I'd made an effort you know, put me face on and wore me best outfit, I stood out like a bulldog's bollock! I don't know what these younger lasses are on, but they were dressed like Worzel Gummidge, baggy kegs, holes in their jumpers, pierced everywhere. Gypoes! Why put lumps of metal in your tongue, or your eyebrow

(*Louder.*) or your fucking clit! Don't make no sense. I know it's fashion, and I did some fucked up stuff in the name of fashion myself, but sniffing tippex while wearing a puffball skirt is a long way from banging a one inch piece of metal in your fadge! So, I'm sat at back in this classroom, and the class is on 'creative approaches to storytelling', I'd missed the induction week cos our Jade was ill. Actually, I don't know why I'm bothering to bullshit you, there were fuck all up with Jade, I'd had me head in a bag of charlie all weekend. Needed to chill out in front of Bargain Hunt and Quincy for a few days! Anyway, this lecturer…I haven't even told you about him, have I? One word. Cunt. End of. So he's on about looking at issues, you know, racism, poverty, teenage mums, drugs, vandalism. Fuck me, I'm waiting for benefit fraud to get a mention, then I've got a full house! And he wants to know how we reckon we could get some ideas going. Well I perked up then. See, I was on this young mums' scheme at Tunstall Road church and we got this visiting theatre group, or actors who can't get a job on telly as I like to call 'em, and they did this thing where we all threw in some ideas and one joey wrote 'em all down on this sheet of paper. Brainstorming, that's what they said it was. So I stick me mitt up and lecturer cunt looks at me. 'Brainstorming,' I sez. 'Very good,' says cunt, and I'm happy as Larry, first time in years a teacher's said very good to me. And I feel that maybe, afterall, I could get along here. So I'm feeling chuffed with me little self when this bitch at front pipes up. 'Excuse me, but the term brainstorming is offensive to people with mental health issues.' (*Pause.*) You fucking what! Spacca, yeah. Flid, mongy, joey, biffa fair does, but fucking brainstorming, you're having a laugh! That was my word, my moment of glory and this scruffy little tart takes it away from me. Who the fuck would find that offensive? Well I were fuming, I kid you not, I felt like walking up to her and slotting her one right on the fucking nose. (*Pause.*) So I did!! (*Pause.*) Maybe try Open University next. (*Exits.*)

DEALER: The worst part of the day, for me, is opening these curtains. (*Goes to window and opens curtains.*) What delights are on display today? (*Looks out.*) I see… shite! Beeston in Bloom! Some people, possibly some of you, open their windows and enjoy the view. Now that would be something. A sprawling garden, with a pond maybe. A lovingly crafted patio with garden furniture and a barbecue. A four by four in black. (*Laughs.*) Do you know all the bus services in Leeds have been given colours? Like the indigo line runs to Armley and the purple line to Headingley, I think. Well some fucker was having a laugh when they named the service to here. The brown line! I kid you not. That's priceless that. Works on so many levels. (*Pause.*) I want to take this opportunity to apologise for all the swearing you're gonna hear, it will be fuck this fuck that and I'm sorry. But, you see, the burglars have been round and they've stolen all the verbs and adjectives and we have to make do. Soz like. (*Pause.*) I won't be talking to you again, until the end, please don't think me rude. (*Rummages under bed and pulls out a chemists bag, checks the contents without showing them to the audience. Hears knock at door, looks at peephole. Sees HARDMAN. Goes to stereo and puts on 'Life on Mars' by David Bowie and opens door.*) Hiya.

HARDMAN: Now then. (*Walks into room, looking around.*)

DEALER: (*Under breath.*) Do come in, please.

HARDMAN: You what?

DEALER: How are you?

HARDMAN: Fucking triffic lad. (*Sits on bed, notices a sorry looking house plant and is temporarily distracted by it.*) Yeah. (*Throughout his time in the room HARDMAN is often distracted by the house plant and looks at it frequently.*)

DEALER: Can I get you owt?

HARDMAN: No.

DEALER: Right.

Long pause, eventually DEALER turns music off.

HARDMAN: Good song.

DEALER: Yeah it is. Before he got shit.

HARDMAN: What you mean?

DEALER: Nineteen eighty-four, death of music, Bowie releases 'Let's Dance'.

HARDMAN: I'm not with you kid.

DEALER: Well it were Ziggy wasn't it? The thin white duke. 'Heroes', 'Spiders from Mars', 'Diamond Dogs' bisexual, pill popping chameleon of rock. Then he marries some supermodel and releases 'Let's Dance'. Ergo, the death of good music.

HARDMAN: It's only a song.

DEALER: True. But I was just trying to make conversation really.

HARDMAN: Oh.

DEALER: (*After long silence.*) What do you want?

HARDMAN: You what?

DEALER: What do you want?

HARDMAN: To walk out of my house without seeing scum.

DEALER: (*Pause.*) You could try keeping your eyes closed.

HARDMAN: (*Gives a silencing look.*) Or?

DEALER: Or…you could…I don't know, I need you to be more specific…define scum.

HARDMAN: Smackheads, thieves, villains, paedophiles, gyppoes...dealers.

DEALER: Right. I'd try staying indoors more, cos they're here to stay.

HARDMAN: Mouthy fucker aren't you?

DEALER: Not really.

HARDMAN: I'm gonna kick the shit out of you in a minute.

DEALER: Say again?

HARDMAN: You heard.

TEENAGE BOY knocks on the window.

DEALER: I'll just get that.

HARDMAN: Fine.

DEALER opens the window to talk to him.

DEALER: So how goes it on the outside world?

TEENAGE BOY: You're not missing owt. Drugs and violence.

DEALER: It were cigarettes and alcohol in my day.

TEENAGE BOY: Proper bored.

DEALER: What you been doing?

TEENAGE BOY: Not been doing owt.

DEALER: Shouldn't you be at school though?

TEENAGE BOY: Nah...excluded.

DEALER: Is that the same as expelled?

TEENAGE BOY: Yeah.

DEALER: What did you do?

TEENAGE BOY: Kicked off, nowt much. (*Pause.*) So, what you up to?

DEALER: Same shit, different day you know?

TEENAGE BOY: Yeah. (*Pause.*) How's business?

DEALER: (*Glances back to HARDMAN.*) Cut-throat.

TEENAGE BOY: (*Trying to look through window.*) Who you got in there?

DEALER: Good question. (*To HARDMAN.*) Who've I got in here?

HARDMAN: None of your fucking business.

DEALER: (*To TEENAGE BOY.*) None of your fucking business.

TEENAGE BOY: Nice. Is he alright?

DEALER: Yeah I think so.

TEENAGE BOY: (*Pause.*) If you need owt doing just let me know.

DEALER: I thought we'd been through this.

TEENAGE BOY: Don't start.

DEALER: I've told you man, you're a bright kid, you don't need to deal.

TEENAGE BOY: (*Sarcastic.*) Yeah, I can do what I want with my life.

DEALER: Yeah.

TEENAGE BOY: The world is my oyster.

DEALER: Yeah.

TEENAGE BOY: So I wanna deal.

DEALER: No.

TEENAGE BOY: Hang on! If I can do anything I want, like you said. Then you shouldn't stop me.

DEALER: I'm not stopping you, I'm being your careers advisor.

TEENAGE BOY: You're being a hypocrite.

DEALER: Yes I am. I am a fucking hypocrite. But you don't want to end up like me.

TEENAGE BOY: How come every adult I know, doesn't want me to end up like them? Me dad don't want me working up ladders all me life, me mum don't want me getting some little bird pregnant, like what happened to her, me brother don't want me on the graft so I end up in nick like him. And you don't want me dealing so I end up like you. What's that all about?

DEALER: They don't want you making the same mistakes.

TEENAGE BOY: But everyone I know regrets their life. So, everyone will make mistakes. So, why don't you all save your breath and let me get on with it, cos my life's gonna be fucked up whatever.

DEALER: (*Pause.*) Like I said before, you're a bright kid. Too fucking bright you little know it all.

TEENAGE BOY: I've got an answer for everything.

DEALER: You just don't know what the question is.

TEENAGE BOY: And you do?

DEALER: I think we've already established that I'm a hypocrite!

TEENAGE BOY: Well thank you Yoda, I have learnt my lesson well.

DEALER: (*Impersonating Yoda.*) Strong is the force in this one.

22

TEENAGE BOY: Sort us a five will you?

DEALER: Piss off!

TEENAGE BOY: I've got it. (*Pulls fiver out of pocket.*) Here.

DEALER: Don't smoke that shit, it dulls the senses.

TEENAGE BOY: I'm bored man.

DEALER: So climb a tree or summat.

TEENAGE BOY: Piss off.

DEALER: It's a nice day…

TEENAGE BOY: No it's not.

DEALER: Go do whatever teenage boys are supposed to do.

TEENAGE BOY: Exactly. Gimme a five.

DEALER: Oh for fuck's sake. (*Gets dope out of his pocket.*) You're wasting your life you know!

TEENAGE BOY: You're supposed to be selling it, not putting people off.

DEALER: (*Bites dope in half and gives one half to TEENAGE BOY.*) It's all part of the service, free counselling session with every purchase.

TEENAGE BOY: You're radged. (*Tries to hand fiver to DEALER.*)

DEALER: That I am. (*Refuses TEENAGE BOY's money.*) Nah, you're okay.

TEENAGE BOY: You sure?

DEALER: Yeah. Fuck it.

TEENAGE BOY: How come?

DEALER: Feeling generous today.

TEENAGE BOY: Cheers man.

DEALER: Not a problem. I'd better get back. (*Nods to HARDMAN.*) company and that.

TEENAGE BOY: Oh right, well I'll see you later on then.

DEALER: Alright. Be good.

TEENAGE BOY: Fuck that.

DEALER: In a bit.

TEENAGE BOY: In a big bit! (*Leaves.*)

DEALER: (*To himself.*) Take care.

Closes window, speaks to HARDMAN.

Sorry about that.

HARDMAN: Not a problem.

Pause. DEALER sits on floor and stares at HARDMAN.

So, you sell to kiddies?

DEALER: Yeah.

HARDMAN: Why?

DEALER: Why not?

HARDMAN glares at him.

You want me to justify it? (*Pause.*) Never gonna happen.

HARDMAN: I've heard you sell smack as well?

DEALER: Yeah. How much you after?

HARDMAN: Do I look like a smackhead?

DEALER: No, you look like a tough mother fucker.

HARDMAN: I am. (*Pause.*) I don't want you selling smack no more. I don't want you selling owt no more. End of.

DEALER: Ah! So now we get down to business. You want me to stop dealing.

HARDMAN: Correct.

DEALER: And you've come here to reason with me?

HARDMAN: Not quite.

DEALER: So what you got planned?

HARDMAN: Shutting your mouth for a start. (*Stands and takes a tyre iron out of his jacket.*)

DEALER: Right.

HARDMAN: You see, this is my area and scumbags like you aren't welcome any more. Not on my patch.

DEALER: Aw no! No, no, no. You've blown it now.

HARDMAN: What you on about?

DEALER: I was genuinely intimidated before. You know, one word answers, cold stare, you were doing well. And now you start spouting cliches! You've just ruined the whole experience for me.

HARDMAN: (*Pause, incredulous.*) Are you tapped in the head or what? I've got a fucking iron bar in my hand!

DEALER: And I respect that, truly I do. But there's no need to get all Charles Bronson, that's all I'm saying.

HARDMAN: I don't think you've got your head round what's happening here.

DEALER: (*Pause.*) No, I have. (*Slowly stands.*) And I'm gonna make it real easy for you.

HARDMAN: You what?

DEALER: Do me good. (*Lowers head.*)

HARDMAN: You don't think I'll fucking do it!

DEALER: (*Lifts head.*) I'm hoping to God you will mate. It's not what I planned, but you have to take your opportunities where you can.

HARDMAN: Don't be calling my bluff!

DEALER: I'm not, come on, get on with it. (*Lowers head.*) I don't like hospitals, so hit me very, very hard.

HARDMAN backs off a bit.

HARDMAN: Don't you fucking…

DEALER: Kill me.

HARDMAN: Shut your mouth! (*Points tyre iron at him.*)

DEALER: (*Lifts head.*) Get the job done. Come on, I want it.

HARDMAN: Stop now.

DEALER: I do though. You wanna kill me and I wanna die. Now do what you were put on this earth for! (*Screaming.*) Do it!!

HARDMAN: I'm not…

DEALER: What you waiting for? Eh? I'm right here. Stop me from dealing then. Heroin mate, I sell heroin. (*Moves towards HARDMAN.*) To kids, I sell to kids.

HARDMAN: (*Shaking his head.*) Back off.

DEALER: (*Moving closer.*) Dirty smack. Filthy. Cut with shit. Dirty needles. To kids mate, to fucking kiddies.

They are practically nose to nose, HARDMAN is glaring at him, DEALER is smiling.

There's no one more deserving than me. (*He takes a step back and lowers his head.*) Please kill me.

HARDMAN: (*Fuming, long pause, then he smashes tyre iron into DEALER's head.*) ARGHHH!

26

Luke / Nathan / Mikey.

DEALER crumples to floor and rolls into the corner, clutching his head, then he is still and silent.

Fuck wi' me! Eh? You don't call my bluff cunt! You see what you fucking get!

He pushes dealer with his foot, nothing. Quieter.

You fucking see? (*Moves closer to him.*) Oi. (*Shakes DEALER.*) Here, don't play fucking dead on me, I'm wise to that shit. (*Bolts up.*) Fuck! (*Walks round room, thinking.*) Fuck, fuck, fuck. (*Stands still, looking at DEALER.*) Shit! Here, stop playing silly cunts now. (*Pause, moves to DEALERand shakes him more violently, then gently, long pause.*) Come on dickhead, wake up!

There is a knock at the door, it's LAP DANCER, with baby in pram.

You're having a fucking laugh. (*Quietly he approaches door and looks through the spyhole.*)

LAP DANCER is looking through it at the same time and sees his eye.

LAP DANCER: Hiya.

HARDMAN: (*Jumps away from door.*) Fuck me.

LAP DANCER: It's me! Come on, I'm in a rush.

HARDMAN: (*Through door.*) He's not here love, gone to shops. Come back in ten minutes.

LAP DANCER: Who are you?

HARDMAN: I'm a mate of his.

LAP DANCER: So you sort me out.

She tries door.

HARDMAN blocks it with his foot.

27

HARDMAN: Whoah hang on!

LAP DANCER: Come on, what you doing?

HARDMAN: Give me a minute.

LAP DANCER: Well hurry up.

HARDMAN: Just give me a minute for fuck's sake.

> *He frantically searches the room, takes blanket off bed and covers DEALERwith it, he then moves some furniture in front of dealer, he then sits on bed, trying to look cool.*

Come in then!

LAP DANCER: (*Enters with pram. Until she takes the speed, LAP DANCER is lethargic, after; animated.*) Thank God! (*Sees HARDMAN.*) Were you having a wank or what?

HARDMAN: Behave. (*Sees her struggling with pram.*) Here. (*Helps her.*)

LAP DANCER: Ta. So where is he?

HARDMAN: Shops. Getting some food.

LAP DANCER: Oh, so he does eat then.

HARDMAN: (*Confused.*) Yeah.

LAP DANCER: Who are you?

HARDMAN: I told you, a mate.

LAP DANCER: (*Looks closely at him.*) Don't I know you?

HARDMAN: No.

LAP DANCER: Are you sure?

HARDMAN: I just said no.

LAP DANCER: I'm only trying to make conversation. (*Pause.*) Fair enough. Sort us out a wrap will you?

HARDMAN: Right. (*Looks around.*) Where's he keep it?

LAP DANCER: I thought you were a mate.

HARDMAN: I am, but I don't know where he keeps it. Alright?

LAP DANCER: Okay. Fucking hell! It's in his trophy. (*Points to shelf.*)

HARDMAN: (*Goes to shelf, and examines the cricket trophy, finally opens it.*) How many?

LAP DANCER: Just one. I'm working tonight.

HARDMAN: (*Hands her a wrap.*) Where'd you work?

LAP DANCER: I'm a lap dancer.

Takes wrap, HARDMAN is just staring at her.

What's up with you?

HARDMAN: Nowt. (*Pause.*) Do you enjoy it?

LAP DANCER: No I fucking don't, it's boring. (*Looks in wrap.*) Here! What you playing at? I'm not a fucking smack head!

HARDMAN: Eh.

LAP DANCER: This is brown, what the fuck you suggesting here?

HARDMAN: (*Affronted.*) I'm sorry, I didn't fucking know. What the fuck do you want?

LAP DANCER: Phet. (*Hands back the wrap.*)

HARDMAN: Jesus! (*Roots through packages.*) Here what's this? (*Passes her another wrap.*)

LAP DANCER: That's more like it.

She goes to table and begins to chop out a line, HARDMAN is looking at baby in pram.

HARDMAN: You're doing it here?

LAP DANCER: (*Engrossed.*) Yeah.

HARDMAN: What about the baby?

LAP DANCER: (*Disapproving look.*) She's trying to cut down.

HARDMAN: Can you not wait till you get home, I'm in a bit of a rush here.

LAP DANCER: I thought you were waiting for him to get back from the shops?

HARDMAN: No, I've got to go to work.

LAP DANCER: Well, I'm done. (*Snorts a line.*) You want one?

HARDMAN: No.

LAP DANCER: Right. (*Packs up the wrap.*) I'll get out of your hair then. (*She goes to pram.*)

HARDMAN: Whoa there! You forgetting summat?

LAP DANCER: Am I?

HARDMAN: (*Holds out his hand.*) It don't grow on trees you know.

LAP DANCER: It's on tick. (*Goes for door.*)

HARDMAN: (*Blocking her way.*) Hang about. I can't just have you taking his stuff without paying.

LAP DANCER: I told you, I get credit.

HARDMAN: How do I know that?

LAP DANCER: I'm fucking telling you.

HARDMAN: Well I'm fucking telling you, you'd better leave that shit here, cos you're not going without paying.

LAP DANCER: What do you care, we have an arrangement, if you are his mate he'd have told you.

HARDMAN: Well he didn't tell me shit, so I don't know shit, so leave it here. Some mate I'd be if I let you swan off with his gear.

LAP DANCER: (*Looks at him quizzically, then smiles.*) You lying bastard, you know exactly what the score is and you want a bit for yourself, don't you?

HARDMAN: What?

LAP DANCER: Well come on then, I've got to get to work. (*She pushes HARDMAN towards the bed.*)

HARDMAN: What you on about? What you doing?

LAP DANCER: Sit down.

He does, she goes to stereo and puts on 'Confide in Me' by Kylie Minogue.

He likes this one. (*Approaches HARDMAN.*) No touching, alright!

HARDMAN: Here, I don't want...

LAP DANCER: Yeah course you don't. (*She starts to dance and slowly removes her clothes.*)

HARDMAN: Wait a minute.

LAP DANCER: (*Puts finger to his mouth suggestively and stares into his eyes, then licks the back of her finger.*) Ssssssh.

She continues, HARDMAN doesn't know what to do, but is captivated, he keeps looking at the pram, the song ends and her seductive act is over, she starts to dress again.

Right, you fucking satisfied? Can I go now?

HARDMAN: (*Nods and mutters.*) Yeah. (*He cannot look in her eyes.*)

LAP DANCER: You okay?

HARDMAN: I'm sound.

LAP DANCER: Was it alright for you?

HARDMAN: Yeah it was sound.

LAP DANCER: I think I've done alright to say I've got a kid.

HARDMAN: Yeah, you have.

LAP DANCER: No stretch marks or owt?

HARDMAN: No you'd never tell.

LAP DANCER: Well cheer up then!

HARDMAN: Right.

LAP DANCER: A lot of blokes do this.

HARDMAN: Do what?

LAP DANCER: Go all cold, it's nowt to be ashamed of, just a bit of fun, you know?

HARDMAN: I know.

LAP DANCER: So chill out.

HARDMAN: I'm chilled.

LAP DANCER: Glad to hear it. Got a cig?

HARDMAN: (*Gets one out for her, doesn't have one himself.*) Here.

LAP DANCER: Cheers. (*Lights it.*) So what do you do then?

HARDMAN: How long you been dancing?

LAP DANCER: Six months or so. Got offered porn work last week.

HARDMAN: Did you now?

LAP DANCER: Yeah, some bloke came into the club, well flash. Offered me two hundred and fifty to do one scene.

HARDMAN: Right. Well I really must…

LAP DANCER: I told him thanks but no thanks, I can earn one-fifty on a Saturday night and no-one touches me. Them boys in porn can have wicked big dicks on 'em, fuck that! Won't be able to put me legs together for a week, and you never know what they're gonna ask you to do, do you?

HARDMAN: I wouldn't know. I'm not exactly an…

LAP DANCER: I was talking to this lass at ours, she's done a film, just one like. A scene with two blokes, both hung like frigging donkeys, she says. They took her all ways, you know. She said she felt sore by the end of it. Well it came to the spunking scene and they were both wanking off in her face and she was all 'ooh yeah' and 'give it to me' and the first one came right, and got her straight in the eye with a bit of jizz! She was fucking blinded! It's salty innit? So it must hurt like a bastard. So she's trying to wipe her eye and these two geezers are firing spunk all over her, and she falls off the bed! Kicks the cameraman and the whole shot's ruined. (*Laughing, looks expectantly at HARDMAN for a reaction.*)

HARDMAN: (*Pause.*) I don't know what to say to that.

LAP DANCER: She never went back for the re-take! Did a runner! (*After thought.*) I don't think she even got paid.

HARDMAN: I take it that speed's doing the business?

LAP DANCER: Oh yeah, nice gear. Tell him it's nice gear for me will you?

HARDMAN: I will. (*Stands to show her out.*)

LAP DANCER: Actually I'll tell him myself, I'll pop by later.

HARDMAN: (*Walking her to door.*) Right. Well, I'd better get a move on myself, I'm gonna be late. Busy, busy, you know.

LAP DANCER: Oh okay. Well, I'm sorry, I was babbling. (*Allowing herself to be led out.*)

HARDMAN: Not a problem. (*Gets door for her.*) I'll make sure to tell him.

LAP DANCER: Yeah do. I never got your name, I'm Jo.

HARDMAN: Er…Thomas.

LAP DANCER: Nice meeting you Tom.

HARDMAN: Yeah triffic. See you then. (*Practically bundles her out, shuts door and rests his head against it; to himself.*) You've got to be fucking kidding me. (*Stays a while, then turns around and notices baby in pram, jumps.*) Fuck me! (*Looks in pram.*) Shit! (*Looks at door, makes towards it, then returns to pram.*) Erm… I'm just gonna get her, don't worry. (*Goes back to door, as he does, LAP DANCER charges though, hitting HARDMAN.*)

LAP DANCER: (*Calm.*) Can you believe me? I'd forget me fucking head if it wasn't screwed on properly. (*Looks in pram, to baby.*) You alright baby! Mummy's a fucking idiot.

HARDMAN is holding door open.

Sorry about that. (*Gets pram and goes through door.*) See you.

HARDMAN: (*Nods, as LAP DANCER exits, he slams door behind her.*) Crazy. Fucking crazy. (*He walks over to*

DEALER.) You fucking arsehole! (*Sits on bed, confused. Puts his head in his hands. A low whine can be heard from him. Unseen by HARDMAN, OLD MAN walks in, approaches DEALER, who sits up to speak to him.*)

OLD MAN: Oh dear.

DEALER: I know, you don't have to say owt.

OLD MAN: Why did you do it?

DEALER: I saw the opportunity, so I took it.

OLD MAN: To be killed?

DEALER: Yeah, well it's much braver than suicide innit?

OLD MAN: I suppose so.

DEALER: Am I dead?

OLD MAN: No, you've been knocked out.

DEALER: Fucking bastard!

OLD MAN: I thought you weren't going to swear, you promised me.

DEALER: Sorry George, it just slipped out.

OLD MAN: That's alright. (*Pause.*) Who is he?

DEALER: No idea. Came round to stop me dealing.

OLD MAN: A crusader!

DEALER: A what?

OLD MAN: A man on a mission.

DEALER: Yeah maybe. Maybe he's a rival dealer, thinning the competition.

OLD MAN: You do need to stop you know.

DEALER: That's what I'm trying to do.

OLD MAN: Dying is a bit extreme though, don't you think?

DEALER: We've been through this George.

OLD MAN: You might appreciate life more if you stopped selling that muck.

DEALER: Oh George please, come on, no lectures today. (*Pause.*) I'm glad you came George.

OLD MAN: Whenever you need me, I'll be there…

DEALER: That's a Micheal Jackson lyric.

OLD MAN: Is it?

DEALER: Yeah. (*Sings.*) 'Whenever you need me, I'll be there. Don't you know baby! I'll be the-re.'

OLD MAN is looking at him blankly.

DEALER stops, shame-faced.

Sorry.

Pause.

OLD MAN looks at him as if he is crazy.

You were saying?

OLD MAN: I was going to say, but I don't know why you should need a soppy old man to talk to.

DEALER: You're not soppy George, you're my rock.

OLD MAN: (*Points to DEALER's head wound.*) I'm not doing a very good job, am I?

DEALER: I'm a lost cause my friend, don't know why you bother.

OLD MAN: I wonder myself sometimes.

DEALER: (*Sighs.*) Oh, I don't know. I've got a dark cloud in me belly. (*Pause.*) Tell me a story.

OLD MAN: A story?

DEALER: Yeah. Something sedate and calm.

OLD MAN: Sedate?

DEALER: Yes please. (*Pause. OLD MAN is thinking.*) Come on George, you're great at stories. I used to love listening to you.

OLD MAN: Shush boy, I'm trying to think.

DEALER: Sorry.

OLD MAN: (*Long pause.*) I remember something that happened just after my mum passed away.

DEALER: You're gonna tell someone who's suicidal about your mum dying!

OLD MAN: No, bare with me, it's rooted in calmness.

DEALER: You sure now?

OLD MAN: Sure I'm sure. (*Moves around the space whilst telling the story.*) My mum had passed and I'd spent the following weeks with a cloud above my head. I couldn't move forward, life held no joy for me, I couldn't look backwards, for the pain of memories. I guess I can sympathise with you here because I felt like dying myself. I'd spent weeks like this. Wondering if she was alright, hoping she was safe and content. I'd practically stopped sleeping, couldn't go to work and spent most of my time walking the streets in a daze.

DEALER: This'd better have a happy ending.

OLD MAN: It won't have an ending at all if you interrupt again! So this one day, I'd been walking, aimlessly, found myself in the countryside. I felt overwhelmingly tired and sat on a bench, on a hill, overlooking the city. There were tears in my eyes and I remember thinking, 'Where are you mum? Where've you been put?' And then, I saw this bird flying upwards. The strangest looking bird I'd ever seen, it drew level with the sun and disappeared.

DEALER: Disappeared?

OLD MAN: No word of a lie. Hand on heart. It took my breath from me. It was the most beautiful thing I had ever seen. Red and gold in colour, had a tail like a peacock.

DEALER: Peacocks can't fly.

OLD MAN: Clever bugger aren't you? It looked like a peacock. But it wasn't.

DEALER: Was it a gay pigeon? (*Laughs.*)

OLD MAN: You're gonna make me swear in a minute!

DEALER: Sorry George, sorry. (*Pause.*) Come on then, don't keep me in suspenders, what was it?

OLD MAN: Feng-huang.

DEALER: (*Stares incredulous.*) You are having a laugh!

OLD MAN: Feng-huang is a mythical Chinese bird, it's the primordial force of the heavens.

DEALER: And it was in Leeds?

OLD MAN: I saw what I saw. I felt calm, I felt like I had gotten the answer to my questions and me mamma was right where she was supposed to be, in heaven.

DEALER: (*Pause.*) Were you on drugs. (*Laughs.*)

OLD MAN: Yes, well I knew it would probably be wasted on you.

DEALER: No. Play fair, it was a lovely story, but, you know. I don't go for all that heaven stuff, and mythical birds 'n that, it's a bit too much for me.

OLD MAN: Whatever, it happened and I thought I'd tell you.

DEALER: Don't be upset with me George, I can't help it. It's how I am.

OLD MAN: (*Angry.*) That's the whole problem with you though, you're a know-it-all that knows nothing. If it's not in three dimensions in front of your face or on the telly, it's rubbish. For that matter, you think everything's rubbish. If you opened your mind a little you might find some hope.

DEALER: Believe me fella, I want hope. But I don't think I'll be seeing any feng huangs in Beeston.

OLD MAN: You're missing the point.

DEALER: Enlighten me.

OLD MAN: All I'm saying is, I was low, very low and I found some hope in an unexpected place. Keep your eyes open. (*Looks at HARDMAN.*) Hope comes in unexpected forms.

DEALER: Who? (*Indicates HARDMAN.*) Him? That frigging nutter!

OLD MAN: Maybe, you never know. I don't know.

DEALER: I'm doubting that George, big-time.

OLD MAN: (*Shaking his head.*) I do despair of you.

DEALER: That makes two of us.

OLD MAN: Well, I'm going to get going. If you've finished ridiculing me?

DEALER: Don't be like that George. I love having you around, you cheer me up.

OLD MAN: I just wish you'd take things seriously, you're in a bad way you know.

DEALER: (*Blunt.*) If I didn't laugh, I'd cry.

OLD MAN: Of course. Tara for now. (*Goes to leave, then stops.*) Ooh now, what is it you like to say? In a bit?

DEALER: Yes George, in a big bit.

OLD MAN: (*Gives confused wave.*) Aye.

OLD MAN leaves.

DEALER lies down under blanket.

HARDMAN: (*Head in hands.*) Fucking. Fuck. (*Looks at DEALER under blanket.*) Fuck! (*He stands and attempts to sort himself out and calm down, appears to have done so, then breaks the façade.*) You fucking knob-head! What… ARGGHH! (*Punches the air, sits back down on bed.*)

DEALER: (*Removing blanket.*) Can you keep it down?

HARDMAN: (*Shocked.*) Shit! (*Jumps off bed.*)

DEALER: It's alright man, I'm cushty. (*Stands groggily.*) Bit of a sore head like.

HARDMAN: (*Trying to compose himself. Looks at DEALER's head wound, which is quite severe.*) Fucking hell.

DEALER: It's nowt man it's cool.

HARDMAN: It's cool! You're one hard-headed bastard you.

DEALER: Thanks. (*He goes to drawer and looks through it.*)

HARDMAN: (*Quiet.*) You sure you're alright?

DEALER: Yeah, sure. I could go for a paracetomol like, but, I'll live. (*Gives in looking through drawer.*) You should've hit me harder. Were you scared?

HARDMAN: Was I fuck!

DEALER: Don't worry fella, I'll not be telling anyone.

HARDMAN: (*Pause.*) Why'd you make me do it?

DEALER: You've caught me on a strange day. Normally, I would've been cowering and kissing your arse. But not today, today I don't give a fuck. (*Pause.*)

HARDMAN: What's so different about today then?

DEALER: (*Open arms and gazing above.*) Today I am somewhat whimsical yet hardened to this world.

HARDMAN: You wanna lay off the products mate, you're head's gone.

DEALER: Not gone sir, quite the opposite. And I don't do drugs. Reality is something to be faced with a clear head, only then can we understand its true horrors.

HARDMAN: You talk like a fucking mental case.

DEALER: Welcome to the asylum!

HARDMAN: You're not wrong there. (*Pause.*) I'll make a move. We'll just forget it, yeah. I'll leave you be. (*Goes to leave.*)

DEALER: Hang on!

HARDMAN: What?

DEALER: I thought you came here with a purpose.

HARDMAN: I did, but…I just wanted to scare you off and I ending up nearly killing you, it's gone a bit pear-shaped.

DEALER: Did someone hire you?

HARDMAN: No. I told you I'm sick of it all, so I'm doing something about it.

DEALER: Noble then?

HARDMAN: You taking the piss?

DEALER: No! I meant it sincerely. I respect that you're doing something about it.

HARDMAN: (*Cynical.*) Do you now?

DEALER: Yeah, straight up, I respect what you're doing.

HARDMAN: But I want to stop people like you.

DEALER: We need stopping. People like me are a cancer mate.

HARDMAN: So why do it?

DEALER: Million dollar question. (*Thinks.*) I don't think I've got the moral fortitude not to.

HARDMAN: Do what.

DEALER: It doesn't bother me enough not to do it. I understand I'm scum, but I can live with it.

HARDMAN: It's your choice.

DEALER: Yeah, I suppose. No excuses. You fancy a cuppa?

HARDMAN: Eh?

DEALER: Tea or coffee. (*Plugs kettle in.*)

HARDMAN: I wasn't planning on staying.

DEALER: I'd like it if you would.

HARDMAN: Why?

DEALER: Dunno. Thought it might be interesting. Tea or coffee?

HARDMAN: (*Hesitates.*) Tea. Two sugars.

He sits on bed.

DEALER busies himself with making tea.

I won't forget today in a long time.

DEALER: Oh it's a never ending roller-coaster of fun round here!

HARDMAN: (*Pause.*) You had a customer.

DEALER: Yeah, I know.

HARDMAN: You saw!

DEALER: No, I heard. Why didn't you just let her go without paying?

HARDMAN: I wish I fucking had of.

DEALER: But you didn't.

HARDMAN: Well for your information, if I'd have let her off without paying she might have sussed something was up. I would have.

DEALER: Did you enjoy her payment method? Cash, visa or minge?

HARDMAN: Fuck off.

DEALER: Come off it! She paid with her hairy chequebook, that can't be bad.

HARDMAN: You might get off on shit like that, but not me. She had a baby with her.

DEALER: What? Can't women be sexy after they've had a kid then?

HARDMAN: Not when the kid's in the same fucking room, no.

DEALER: But you still let her.

HARDMAN: Yeah.

DEALER: I thought it bothered you?

HARDMAN: Well course it bothered me, but I'm a bloke aren't I? (*Pause.*) Did you hear the shit she was coming out with? Fucking pornos and that!

43

DEALER: Yeah, she's not shy.

HARDMAN: She's filth mate. If she were my daughter I'd wash her mouth out with soap.

DEALER: Well, be grateful she's not.

HARDMAN: I am! What the fuck is up with lassies these days? Getting their bits out for drugs and talking like blokes on a building site. It's a fucking disgrace.

DEALER: I'm as confused as you mate. (*Gives tea.*) Here.

HARDMAN: Ta. (*Sips.*) I think you're the first person I've beaten up then had a cup of tea with.

DEALER: Very civilised of us, innit?

HARDMAN: Yeah.

They both sit in silence, drinking tea.

DEALER: I think she liked you.

HARDMAN: Fuck off!

DEALER: Yeah she did!

HARDMAN: You reckon?

DEALER: Yeah, she didn't want to leave did she?

HARDMAN: She were speeding her tits off, just wanted someone to talk at.

DEALER: Well, maybe.

HARDMAN: (*Pause.*) She's a good-looking lass.

DEALER: Aye, she is.

HARDMAN: Fucking waster though.

DEALER: Aye. (*They drink.*) I think you'd be good for her.

HARDMAN: How?

DEALER: Put her on the straight and narrow. Show her the error of her ways.

HARDMAN: That'd be a challenge!

DEALER: Not half. (*They chuckle.*) She said she was coming back?

HARDMAN: Yeah.

DEALER: Hang around then, see if she does.

HARDMAN: Don't know about that.

DEALER: Why not? It won't do any harm, or have you got other villains to deal with today?

HARDMAN: No, it's nowt like that. I just feel a bit…
I didn't come here to…you know.

DEALER: Don't be daft! It's cool. You've told me what you came round to tell me and now we're just two blokes, chilling out.

HARDMAN: Did you listen to me though?

DEALER: Course I did, you said it loud enough. (*Indicates head wound.*)

HARDMAN: (*Smiles.*) So you gonna stop?

DEALER: (*Thinks.*) I'll make you a promise. You hang around here for a bit and, come tomorrow, I'll knock it on the head.

HARDMAN: You serious?

DEALER: Yeah, why not? I'll try owt once.

HARDMAN: It's a deal matey. I wish you'd have said that before I had to clock you one though.

DEALER: I think I needed it.

HARDMAN: (*Pause.*) Okay. (*Looks at plant.*) But you have to do one other thing for me.

DEALER: What do you want me to do?

HARDMAN: Water this fucking plant before it turns to dust.

DEALER: You serious?

HARDMAN: Course I'm fucking serious, the poor thing's dying here.

DEALER: Your wish is my command. (*Goes to sink to get a glass of water.*)

HARDMAN: Are you really gonna quit dealing?

DEALER: (*Concentrating on watering plant.*) Yeah.

HARDMAN: Why?

DEALER: What's it matter why? I'm gonna stop.

HARDMAN: Fair enough.

DEALER: You like plants then?

HARDMAN: Used to work at a nursery, when I left school.

DEALER: Weren't the kiddies scared of you?

HARDMAN: Funny fucker. A garden centre.

DEALER: Oh right. Why did you leave then if you liked it so much.

HARDMAN: None of your business.

DEALER: True. (*Finishes watering.*) So why do you like plants so much?

HARDMAN: They don't talk shit!

Long pause.

DEALER: I think you're a super-hero.

HARDMAN: (*Laughs unexpectedly.*) You fucking what?

DEALER: No. Hear me out. I don't mean like Superman or Spider-man, I'm not suggesting you've special powers or ought, no, you're more like a Batman character.

HARDMAN: I'm Batman!

DEALER: I'm not saying you are Batman. But think about it, he was a normal bloke who decided, enough is enough, I'm gonna clean the streets. You've stopped me from peddling poison. Play your cards right and you might stop Jo doing drugs and getting her tits out. You, my friend, are saving society!

HARDMAN: But Batman did it for revenge. The Joker killed his family.

DEALER: Revenge was his reason and I'm not saying you are Batman. But there are similarities.

HARDMAN: You talk some nonsense.

DEALER: Why? You tell me that what you're doing isn't like a crime-fighting hero?

HARDMAN: (*Thinks, for a long time.*) Shut up.

DEALER: See. Point proven.

HARDMAN: I ain't a hero kid, I've done my share of shit in the past.

DEALER: Exactly, you're a modern day super-hero, fuelled by guilt and regret, you're paying back your debt to society.

HARDMAN: I'm just doing what I think's right.

DEALER: What happened?

HARDMAN: Eh?

DEALER: What made you think, 'Right, I'm gonna sort this shit-hole out?'

HARDMAN: Can't remember.

DEALER: Come on! You can tell me.

HARDMAN: It was nowt really.

DEALER: I wanna know.

HARDMAN: (*Hard.*) Let it drop.

DEALER: Okay.

Long pause, he laughs.

You're drinking tea with a dealer!

HARDMAN: Aye! But, a soon to be ex-dealer.

DEALER: You're a fucking crime-fighting super-hero you.

HARDMAN: If you say so.

DEALER: Must be nice.

HARDMAN: What must?

DEALER: To be big enough to do whatever you like. So no-one fucks with you.

HARDMAN: Yeah, it's fucking triffic. I have a God-given talent for shitting people up, so I might as well start using for something good.

DEALER: Yeah?

HARDMAN: Yeah. I've made some mistakes, but fuck it.

DEALER: Have you?

HARDMAN: Course I have, but fuck it.

DEALER: Fuck it! I like that.

There's a knock at the door.

HARDMAN: Customer.

DEALER: Might be her. (*Knowing smile.*)

HARDMAN: So what if it is? I don't give a fuck.

DEALER: Course you don't.

HARDMAN: I don't.

DEALER: (*Goes to door.*) What if it's a smackhead? You gonna behave?

HARDMAN: (*Thinks.*) Yeah.

Opens door, it's LAP DANCER.

DEALER: Babycakes!

LAP DANCER: (*Hugs and kisses him.*) Now then you little ugly bastard!

DEALER: Come in gorgeous.

She does and sees HARDMAN.

LAP DANCER: Hello again.

HARDMAN: Hi.

Awkward pause.

Meanwhile, OLD MAN has appeared at the door.

OLD MAN: (*To DEALER.*) What's that on your face?

DEALER: (*Touching his face.*) What's what?

OLD MAN: There, (*Nods.*) below your nose.

DEALER: (*Touches top lip.*) What you on about old man?

OLD MAN: Your frown is upside down!

DEALER: Funny bugger.

OLD MAN exits, laughing.

DEALER turns to LAP DANCER.

How's my favourite bitch?

LAP DANCER: Hunky dory, thanks for asking.

DEALER: So, to what do I owe this pleasure?

LAP DANCER: No reason, you were out before, so I thought I'd pop back to say hello.

DEALER: Hello.

LAP DANCER: Hello. (*They laugh.*) Anyway, what's wi' you leaving your room. Getting brave in your old age?

DEALER: (*Glances at HARDMAN.*) Well, you know, I'll try owt once.

LAP DANCER: And how was the outside world?

DEALER: (*Beat.*) Drugs and violence.

LAP DANCER: (*To HARDMAN.*) And how is Thomas?

HARDMAN: Sound love. You?

LAP DANCER: Sound is good. (*To DEALER.*) I'm spitting feathers though!

DEALER: Sorry baby. You want a coffee?

LAP DANCER: Got owt stronger?

DEALER: (*Thinks.*) I've got some gin stashed for emergencies, nowt to mix it with though.

LAP DANCER: (*To HARDMAN.*) He's a crap host in't he?

HARDMAN: He is, yeah.

LAP DANCER: (*To DEALER.*) As it comes is fine.

DEALER: Okey dokey. (*To HARDMAN.*) You want?

HARDMAN: Aye I will. Cheers.

DEALER goes to get gin and three glasses; to LAP DANCER.

You want to sit down? (*Stands.*)

LAP DANCER: Cheers Thomas.

Sits on bed.

HARDMAN is stood uncomfortably.

Not many places to sit in here is there?

HARDMAN: No, not really.

DEALER: (*Looking for gin.*) You two slating my room?

LAP DANCER: Shut up bitch! (*To HARDMAN.*) Here, I'll scooch up. (*Does.*)

HARDMAN: Cheers. (*Sits on bed with LAP DANCER.*) Where's the nipper?

LAP DANCER: Left her in a phone box.

HARDMAN doesn't know how to react.

Her dad's got her for ten minutes.

HARDMAN: He's still around then?

LAP DANCER: We're not together. But he'll have her every now and then. Don't trust him to have her long though.

HARDMAN: Why not?

LAP DANCER: Fucking pisshead, isn't he?

HARDMAN: Right.

LAP DANCER: (*Pause.*) I felt a bit embarrassed.

HARDMAN: What about?

51

LAP DANCER: When I was round here before, you know. I got outside and thought about it. (*Covers face with hand, jokingly.*) The fucking shame!

HARDMAN: (*Laughing.*) Don't worry about it love.

LAP DANCER: I bet you thought you'd got a right one here though.

HARDMAN: (*Smiling.*) I'll admit I was little thrown by the porno story.

LAP DANCER: Sorry.

HARDMAN: And the lap dance.

LAP DANCER: Sorry.

HARDMAN: And the baby being in the room.

LAP DANCER: You're taking the piss now! Shut up!

HARDMAN: It's alright though, no harm done.

LAP DANCER: Good, well as long as I didn't freak you out.

HARDMAN: Nah, never.

LAP DANCER: (*Touches his leg affectionately.*) You're alright you Thomas.

HARDMAN: (*Quiet.*) I'm beginning to think so.

DEALER: (*With drinks.*) Here you go then children. (*Hands drinks out.*) Don't be spilling it on me bed though.

LAP DANCER: Nice one.

HARDMAN: Cheers.

LAP DANCER: (*Goes to take a drink, then notices DEALER's head wound.*) What's that? (*Points to DEALER's head.*)

DEALER: What's what?

LAP DANCER: That huge fucking crater on your head!

DEALER: Observant aren't you?

LAP DANCER: What is it?

DEALER: A huge fucking crater on me head.

LAP DANCER: (*Grabs DEALER to look closer.*) Come here.

DEALER: Gerroff, it hurts.

LAP DANCER: Shut up you puff! (*Looks closer.*) Jesus Christ! You been chasing parked cars?

DEALER: (*Pulling away.*) Don't put your fucking finger in it!

LAP DANCER: Stop being a nancy. How'd you do that? (*Looks at HARDMAN who is trying to ignore the conversation.*) How'd he do that?

DEALER: I fell.

LAP DANCER: Yeah course you did. You'd better get to casualty.

DEALER: No, it's all right.

LAP DANCER: It needs stitching.

DEALER: Nah.

LAP DANCER: Don't be stupid.

DEALER: I don't do hospitals.

LAP DANCER: It'll get infected.

HARDMAN: Stop mithering him.

LAP DANCER: You shut up! (*To DEALER.*) Go!

DEALER: I'm not going anywhere.

LAP DANCER: Well get me some antiseptic and a bandage, I'll sort it for you.

DEALER: I haven't got none. Just leave it.

LAP DANCER: Then get to the chemists and buy some! I mean it.

DEALER: The fucking chemists! That's worse than the hospital.

LAP DANCER: How is it?

DEALER: Full of druggies getting methadone.

LAP DANCER: Stop being stubborn and get me a bandage.

DEALER: There's nothing wrong with me!

HARDMAN: She's right you know. You should get it cleaned and covered.

DEALER: Don't back her up!

LAP DANCER: (*Pointing to door.*) Go get it dealt with.

DEALER: (*Thinks.*) I'll see if old biddy next door's got a bandage, all right?

LAP DANCER: Yes!

DEALER: (*Muttering.*) Who d'you think you are? Me fucking mother.

LAP DANCER: You what?

DEALER: Nothing darling. You two gonna play nice when I'm gone?

LAP DANCER: Fuck off will you!

He leaves. Long, awkward silence.

How'd he do that?

HARDMAN: (*Thinks.*) I did it.

LAP DANCER: Eh?

HARDMAN: Yeah, we had a…misunderstanding. It's alright now though.

LAP DANCER: Glad to hear it, I'll make sure I never piss you off!

HARDMAN: It was an accident. (*Long pause.*) He's alright though int he?

LAP DANCER: Yeah, he's sweet.

HARDMAN: Bit weird though.

LAP DANCER: A bit?

HARDMAN: What's the score with him?

LAP DANCER: He gets these things…attacks like. He just kinda freaks out and gets scared.

HARDMAN: Why?

LAP DANCER: Dunno, he's fucking depressed as well. Most times I come round here, he just grunts at me. It's like getting blood out of a stone. He's better today than I've seen him in a long time.

HARDMAN: That bump on the head must've done him good.

LAP DANCER: (*Laughs.*) Yeah. (*Pause.*) He thinks too much, that's his problem. (*Gets wrap out of trophy.*) You fancy a line?

HARDMAN: Don't touch it.

LAP DANCER: Right. Do you mind if I have one?

HARDMAN: (*Thinks.*) Do you need one?

LAP DANCER: Just a bit of fun innit?

HARDMAN stands and puts glass in sink.

What's up?

HARDMAN: Nothing.

LAP DANCER: Have I pissed you off?

HARDMAN: No. (*Stays by sink.*)

LAP DANCER: (*Looking for a wrap.*) Don't like drugs, do you?

HARDMAN: I used to put that shit on me cornflakes years back.

LAP DANCER: Why'd you stop?

HARDMAN: Cos it's shit innit?

LAP DANCER: Makes me feel good.

HARDMAN: Knock yourself out then.

LAP DANCER: No, I don't wanna, not if it's gonna fuck you off.

HARDMAN: It's your choice, you're a big girl.

LAP DANCER: That's not something you should say to a lady!

HARDMAN: Sorry. You're not a big girl in that way.

LAP DANCER: Thank you. (*Pause, puts wrap away.*)

HARDMAN: I don't wanna make you feel bad about it.

LAP DANCER: Too late.

HARDMAN: Well, I'm glad you're not.

LAP DANCER: You're a dying breed. Even me mam'll have a bit of speed at the weekened.

HARDMAN: Your mam?

LAP DANCER: Yeah, she says she doesn't get as pissed if she has a couple of dabs.

HARDMAN: I could not imagine my old dear on speed.

LAP DANCER: Come and sit back down. The dirty drugs have gone.

HARDMAN: Okay.

Sits on bed, awkward silence, LAP DANCER is staring at him.

LAP DANCER: You got right nice eyes you.

HARDMAN: Cheers.

LAP DANCER: (*Pause.*) You don't have to say something nice back, it's alright!

HARDMAN: Sorry, fucking hell! (*Pause.*)

LAP DANCER: Well go on then!

HARDMAN: I'm thinking.

LAP DANCER: If you have to think about it, you obviously can't find owt nice to say.

HARDMAN: Course I can! You putting me under pressure though aren't you?

LAP DANCER: (*Joking.*) You're hurting my feelings here. (*Pretends to cry.*)

HARDMAN: Behave yourself. (*Thinks.*) You've got a nice face.

LAP DANCER: Nice! That's fucking great that. Ooh, don't I feel special.

HARDMAN: I'm shit with words! Alright, it's not nice…

LAP DANCER: That's even worse!

HARDMAN: (*Puts hand up to shut her up.*) It's clean. You've got a clean face. Like, in the magazines, they have to fanny about with the pictures to make the women look right. But, I don't think they'd have to with you.

LAP DANCER: (*Puts hand to mouth.*) Bless you.

HARDMAN: You happy now?

LAP DANCER: You are just the sweetest thing!

HARDMAN: Don't be telling anyone, you'll ruin my rep.

LAP DANCER: Do you mean it?

HARDMAN: I don't say owt I don't mean.

LAP DANCER: I'd remember that line if I were you. That'd proper get you into any lass's knickers.

HARDMAN: I didn't say it to get in your knickers.

LAP DANCER: Shame. (*Her mobile rings.*) Great timing! (*She looks at phone, to HARDMAN.*) It's her dad. (*Takes call.*) What!?

The rest of the phone conversation is silent.

DEALER has got a bandage and is stood outside door, listening in.

OLD MAN sneaks up behind him.

OLD MAN: You'll never hear owt good of yourself, listening in.

DEALER: (*Jumps.*) You devious old sod!

OLD MAN: (*Laughing.*) How's it going in there?

DEALER: Not sure. (*Resumes his listening post.*) I think she's on the phone.

OLD MAN: Is that good?

DEALER: I wouldn't have thought so.

OLD MAN: How you doing?

DEALER: (*Stands to face him.*) I'm good.

OLD MAN: I'm gobsmacked. Don't think I've heard you say that for a while.

DEALER: I've not have I? I do though, I feel good.

OLD MAN: (*Pause.*) So, who is he?

DEALER: Got myself a modern day, crime-fighting super-hero!

OLD MAN: Have you now?

DEALER: Yeah.

OLD MAN: But aren't you a criminal?

DEALER: I was, not any more. Fate has brought us together.

OLD MAN: You do talk some nonsense!

DEALER: Don't you be putting a downer on me.

OLD MAN: I'm not, I'm happy for you. So where does Joanne fit in to all this?

DEALER: Glamorous assistant maybe?

OLD MAN: (*Long pause.*) So, no more suicide talk then.

DEALER: I hope not. (*Pause.*) It's weird.

OLD MAN: What is?

DEALER: I've always thought people like him were just brain-dead, townie wankers.

OLD MAN: Is he not then?

DEALER: No. I think he used to be. But not now. He's using his powers for the common good!

OLD MAN: That's how it should be.

DEALER: I wanted him to kill me and it ends up he shows me the way forward.

OLD MAN: And how has he done that?

DEALER: (*Opens door to see LAP DANCER on phone and HARDMAN nonchalantly watching her.*) Look at him! He's never had a doubt about himself in his life! If he wants to do something, he does it. Wham! If he wants something, he takes it. Ker-pow! If someone pisses him off he sorts it. Blam! (*Shuts door.*) I've got it wrong George. Sitting in me room all these years, brooding about how shit it all is, how people are shit. What I should've been doing is living and stop worrying about it.

OLD MAN: Nice thought.

DEALER: You seem doubtful George.

OLD MAN: Not at all. No. I just want you to be cautious. I know how much you want to be better, I've seen you go through it all, remember? And I'd hate to see you get disappointed.

DEALER: When your opinion of the human race is as low as mine, it's difficult to be disappointed.

OLD MAN: Good point. Well put.

DEALER: Thank you. (*Puts hand to OLD MAN's head.*) I'll be fine George, I know what I want now.

OLD MAN: Which is what?

DEALER: To be better. And to do that, I'm gonna have to be strong, like him.

OLD MAN: Physically strong?

DEALER: Start with the body and the mind will follow.

OLD MAN: I'm looking out for you kid.

DEALER: I know, and believe me, I'd be long dead if it wasn't for you. You're my guardian angel, aren't you?

OLD MAN: I'm happy to be your angel, young sir. You'd best get back to your company. I'll see you soon. (*Goes to leave.*)

DEALER: Thanks George.

OLD MAN leaves.

LAP DANCER: (*Back in room, still on phone, now shouting.*) Well fuck you then, you fucking crank! You can't do one thing for me? I never ask fuck all of you. (*Pause.*) Bollocks to you. I'll get her now. (*Beat.*) You fuck off! (*Switches phone off, to HARDMAN.*) Sorry bout that.

HARDMAN: You okay?

LAP DANCER: Yeah, just that knobhead can't look after Jade, probably needs to get pissed. I'm gonna have to go.

HARDMAN: Oh, okay.

LAP DANCER: Shame.

HARDMAN: What is?

LAP DANCER: I was enjoying me little self. I love me baby to death, but it's nice to have some time off.

HARDMAN: I think that's alright.

LAP DANCER: Yeah. Right. Well I'll be off then. (*Doesn't move.*)

HARDMAN: Okay. Right. Take care of yourself love.

LAP DANCER: I will. (*Hesitant.*) See you Thomas.

HARDMAN: Yeah, see you.

LAP DANCER leaves and bundles into DEALER.

Bollocks.

LAP DANCER: (*To DEALER.*) Out me road you!

DEALER: You off baby?

LAP DANCER: Yeah, gotta get Jade.

DEALER: Alright, well, take care, cos we care!

LAP DANCER: I will. (*Whispers.*) If he asks you can give him my number.

DEALER: No probs.

LAP DANCER leaves.

DEALER enters room.

What did you say to her?

HARDMAN: Fuck all! She had to go.

DEALER: She was crying.

HARDMAN: Was she?

DEALER: No! She said to give you her number.

HARDMAN: (*Trying to stay cool.*) Right.

DEALER: Result eh?

HARDMAN: Yeah.

DEALER: Don't be too happy, you might smile.

HARDMAN: What's that supposed to mean?

DEALER: Dunno. Just sounded cool. (*Pause.*) Well I don't have to bother with this now. (*Throws bandage on bed.*)

HARDMAN: Yes you do.

DEALER: Eh?

HARDMAN: Your head's fucked fella, you need to get that on it.

DEALER: I need more than a bandage to stop my head from being fucked.

HARDMAN: Go on, get it sorted.

DEALER: I can't do it myself, you'll have to.

HARDMAN: Behave, do I look like a nurse?

DEALER: (*Looks at him.*) I'm just trying to picture you in the uniform!

HARDMAN: Well fucking don't. (*Picks up bandage.*) Where's the antiseptic?

DEALER: What?

HARDMAN: The antiseptic. You can't just slap a bandage on it knobhead.

DEALER: I forgot to ask.

HARDMAN: You're fucking thick you. (*Grabs bottle of gin.*) This'll do. Get over sink.

DEALER: You gonna pour that on me?

HARDMAN: Yeah.

DEALER: You having a laugh?

HARDMAN: Am I smiling?

DEALER: No.

HARDMAN: Then I'm being serious, get your arse over here.

DEALER goes to sink.

This'll fucking hurt.

HARDMAN unceremoniously pours gin over his head wound.

DEALER: (*Screaming.*) YOU MOTHER FUCKING...
 JESUS CHRIST!!!

HARDMAN: (*Laughing.*) Shut up you puff!

DEALER: It's in me fucking eyes!

HARDMAN: It won't kill you.

DEALER: Feels like it! Pass me a towel.

HARDMAN: (*Laughing, passes him a towel.*) That were fun.

DEALER: Fucking sadist. (*Presses towel to his face.*) I smell
 like a frigging wino now.

HARDMAN: Here, sit down you faggot.

He does. HARDMAN unravels the bandage.

Put your finger on it.

DEALER puts his finger on the wound and yelps in pain.

Not the cut you idiot, the bandage, put your finger on
 the bandage.

DEALER: Well you should've said.

He holds bandage in place.

*HARDMAN concentrates hard on getting the bandage wrapped
 on.*

What did you talk about?

HARDMAN: None of your business.

DEALER: Do you like her?

HARDMAN: She's all right.

DEALER: Fuck off! All right? I've seen her naked as well,
 you know.

HARDMAN: So's half of Leeds. (*Pause.*) I'm making a right balls of this.

DEALER: You should've left it rolled up.

HARDMAN: It's too late to say that now. (*Goes back to concentrating.*) I might have to start again.

DEALER: I think you should.

HARDMAN removes bandage and starts to roll up.

Long pause.

HARDMAN: (*Whilst bandaging.*) I were watching the news. Local news like. It went: shooting, missing kiddy, rape, school closure, old age pensioner getting mugged, couple of robberies and a drugs clampdown.

DEALER is just listening.

I'd say half of em were within two miles of here. (*Pause.*) The last story, you know the 'and finally' story, always funny or soppy, was this little duckling who'd been orphaned by some kids killing its mum. This gadger found it and took it home. He had this sheep-dog at home and now the dog's taken the duckling in like, you know, bringing it up as it's own. It made me...cry. (*Pause.*) I love animals. Especially dogs. But I'd just sat through all the human stories and felt fuck all. That isn't right. We shouldn't get used to shit like that. (*Pause.*) So I gets thinking, maybe I can do summat about it. (*Pause.*) You wanted to know.

DEALER: (*Soft.*) I've got a proposition for you.

HARDMAN: What?

DEALER: I wanna be like you.

End of Act One.

ACT TWO

Two weeks later. Same room but contents have changed slightly. Resembles a gymnasium, weights and exercise equipment everywhere. DEALER is working out. Loud music is playing (Rage Against the Machine or Limp Bizkit). TEENAGE BOY is knocking on window. DEALER is oblivious. DEALER has taken on some of the HARDMAN's characteristics.

TEENAGE BOY: (*Shouts.*) Oi! (*Knocks.*) 'Ere come on!

> *He opens window and climbs in.*
>
> *DEALER is still oblivious.*
>
> *TEENAGE BOY turns off the music.*
>
> *DEALER carries on regardless.*

You deaf or what?

DEALER: (*Stops and looks at him.*) Where you been?

TEENAGE BOY: Scarborough. What you up to?

DEALER: Training. What were you doing in Scarborough?

TEENAGE BOY: Ran away. What you training for?

DEALER: Can't tell. What you run away for?

TEENAGE BOY: Me old man caught me with some Es. Had to let him calm down.

DEALER: And has he?

TEENAGE BOY: Has he fuck! (*Petulant.*) Miserable old bastard.

DEALER: (*Grabbing a towel.*) Why don't you ever use the door?

TEENAGE BOY: (*Shrugs.*) Dunno. (*Picks up a dumb-bell.*) What's all this about then?

DEALER: Bit nosey for a nobody, aren't you?

TEENAGE BOY: Just asking.

DEALER: Well don't.

TEENAGE BOY: What's up wi' you?

DEALER: Come again?

TEENAGE BOY: What you being all arsey for?

DEALER: You just climbed in through my window and disturbed me.

TEENAGE BOY: It never bothered you before.

DEALER: I didn't care what happened before.

TEENAGE BOY: Well… I'm sorry.

DEALER: Good.

Pause.

TEENAGE BOY is awkward.

What was Scarborough like?

TEENAGE BOY: Shit.

DEALER: Why?

TEENAGE BOY: Dunno, just was. I used to like it when I was on holiday, but it fucking sucked.

DEALER: Off-season.

TEENAGE BOY: Yeah.

DEALER: Seaside towns have higher suicide rates.

TEENAGE BOY: Not surprised.

Pause.

DEALER is confidently waiting for TEENAGE BOY to speak.

I'm proper sorry I disturbed you.

DEALER: I'll let you off.

TEENAGE BOY: So…you alright then?

DEALER: Ticketty Boo.

TEENAGE BOY: What you been up to?

DEALER: Getting my shit together.

TEENAGE BOY: Right.

Pause.

DEALER gets a drink of water.

Can I score?

DEALER: No.

TEENAGE BOY: Oh come on. I've got money.

DEALER: I said no.

TEENAGE BOY: Why not?

DEALER: I don't deal.

TEENAGE BOY: You what! Stop pissing about.

DEALER: I'm not pissing about. I don't deal.

TEENAGE BOY: You do. That's what you do.

DEALER: Not any more.

TEENAGE BOY: Why not?

DEALER: That's not your business.

TEENAGE BOY: Fucking hell! So what you doing for cash?

DEALER: I've put by. (*Pause.*) Look, I'm a bit busy…

TEENAGE BOY: Right…no problem. I'll fuck off. It's just…

DEALER: What?

TEENAGE BOY: No, it's okay.

DEALER: What?

TEENAGE BOY: I'm a bit stuck for somewhere to stay.

DEALER: Go home.

TEENAGE BOY: I can't. He won't have me back.

DEALER: I can't help you.

TEENAGE BOY: Okay.

Pause.

DEALER: I really can't. I'm not being a cunt.

TEENAGE BOY: I know. It's cool.

DEALER: Look, you just gotta bite the bullet and go home.
    Get it over and done with.

TEENAGE BOY: Yeah, I suppose.

DEALER: Sort it out.

TEENAGE BOY: Yeah.

DEALER: I couldn't let you stop here.

TEENAGE BOY: It's alright.

DEALER: I would if I could.

TEENAGE BOY: I know. I'll get off then. (*Goes to leave via
    window.*) In a bit!

DEALER: You gonna be alright?

TEENAGE BOY: (*Stops.*) I'll be cool. Nowt new, is it?

DEALER: Suppose not. (*Pause.*) If your old fella gives you
    any shit, just let me know.

TEENAGE BOY: (*Thinks he's joking.*) Yeah right. (*Realises DEALER is being serious.*) You mean it?

DEALER: (*Posturing, but still looking feeble.*) Course I fucking mean it! Just give me a nod, alright?

TEENAGE BOY: (*Trying to hide his amusement.*) Right.

DEALER: Here, wait up. (*Goes to a cupboard, takes out large bag of weed.*) Got some leftovers.

TEENAGE BOY: Fuck me! How much is there.

DEALER: Couple of nine bars. (*Grabs a handful.*) Here, (*Stuffs it in TEENAGE BOY's pocket.*) don't say I never give you ought.

TEENAGE BOY: You're a life saver.

DEALER: That's the idea.

TEENAGE BOY: (*Indicating bag.*) What you gonna do with the rest?

DEALER: Not sure. (*Puts it back in cupboard.*)

TEENAGE BOY: Cheers mate.

DEALER: Not a problem kid. You be good.

TEENAGE BOY: (*Leaves.*) In a bit.

DEALER: In a big bit.

He puts music on, The Source feat. Candi Staton – 'You Got the Love', and returns to working out.

After a while OLD MAN enters room.

DEALER is about to do sit-ups.

OLD MAN stands directly in his eyeline as DEALER does first sit-up.

Aargh!

OLD MAN: (*Over loud music.*) Sorry.

DEALER: (*Goes to turn music off.*) Jesus fucking Christ, can a man not get a minute to himself! (*Turns music off.*)

OLD MAN: Did I disturb you?

DEALER: Just a bit. (*Pause.*) Why you here?

OLD MAN: No reason. Just thought I'd say hello.

DEALER: Really?

OLD MAN: Yeah, I've not seen you in a while and I thought we could catch up.

DEALER: That's not why you're here at all.

OLD MAN: (*Laughs.*) No, not at all. What's going on with you, I'm worried.

DEALER: Well I'm not. Never felt better.

OLD MAN: Is that right?

DEALER: Course it is. I've not had any attacks, have I? I feel focussed...stronger. Why is that owt to worry about?

OLD MAN: No, I agree, you've not been poorly for a while now. But I want to know why you're being so off with everyone?

DEALER: I'm not being off!

OLD MAN: (*Softly.*) Yes you are.

DEALER: No. What I'm being, is a man, for once.

OLD MAN: I'm a man aren't I? Shall I start being rude? I might have to go find someone to beat up soon.

DEALER: If you like, I don't care. (*Goes back to working out.*)

OLD MAN: I'm pleased you feel better.

DEALER: Sounds like it.

OLD MAN: I just think you could feel better, nicer.

DEALER: Is this about the kid? (*Indicates window.*) Some little joyriding junkie, I couldn't have him staying here.

OLD MAN: I thought your new lease of life included helping people.

DEALER: Stopping people, not helping. Once enough have been stopped, then everybody's gonna be happy.

OLD MAN: Yes. Everybody.

DEALER: I'm not listening to you. Take your lecture elsewhere cos I'm sound me.

Pause.

OLD MAN stares intently at DEALER.

Do you want me to go back to being suicidal? Is that it?

OLD MAN: You're being silly now.

DEALER: Am I? Now I'm alright, you're a bit redundant aren't you? You were happier when I needed you.

OLD MAN: You're talking nonsense. I'm just…

DEALER: Leaving, is what you're just. You remind me of being ill, and that has no place in my life anymore. You want to be here, support what I'm doing.

OLD MAN: I'm not sure I can condone what you're doing.

DEALER: Then, that's that. Job done. Thanks for all you've done for me in the past, I mean that, I really appreciate it, but I'm in a different place now. And my needs are different.

OLD MAN: (*Pause.*) If you're sure.

DEALER looks defiant.

That's me then.

DEALER: (*Softly.*) No regrets.

OLD MAN: No. I'm glad for you…

HARDMAN and LAP DANCER burst through door, in high spirits.

OLD MAN stays to watch for a minute then leaves.

HARDMAN: Now then, mini-me!

DEALER: Now then big fella. How's tricks?

LAP DANCER: Hello you ugly little bastard.

DEALER: (*Nods.*) Gorgeous.

HARDMAN: (*Sits on bed and pats it for LAP DANCER to join him.*) Been training?

DEALER: Yeah. Hard.

LAP DANCER: You can't tell.

DEALER: You will soon.

HARDMAN: (*To LAP DANCER.*) Leave mini-me alone. He's doing alright. Gonna be big and strong like his daddy. (*To DEALER.*) Aren't you?

DEALER: Course I am.

HARDMAN: You eating right.

DEALER: Steak, malt bread and fruit.

HARDMAN: Good lad.

LAP DANCER: (*To DEALER.*) You got any speed love?

DEALER: (*Looks at HARDMAN for guidance.*) I'm not…

HARDMAN: I told her you had some stock left over.

DEALER: Yeah but it's just…

HARDMAN: Mates innit? That's not dealing. We had a heavy one last night (*To LAP DANCER.*) didn't we?

LAP DANCER: Not half! (*To DEALER.*) We just want sommat to keep us going till tonight.

HARDMAN: Can't be sleeping through the day. Got stuff to do haven't we?

DEALER: Right.

HARDMAN: So, stop being a tight cunt and get the billy out.

DEALER: (*Confused.*) Okay. (*Goes to trophy.*) Didn't think you touched it.

HARDMAN: Every now and then don't hurt, do it?

DEALER: No. (*Hands wrap to HARDMAN, he doesn't take it.*)

HARDMAN: Ladies first.

DEALER: (*Hands wrap to LAP DANCER.*) Here you go.

LAP DANCER: Cheers babe. (*She goes to worktop to chop two lines out.*)

DEALER: (*To HARDMAN.*) So, you alright then?

HARDMAN: Yeah cushty. (*Secretive.*) Need a word with you later.

DEALER: Sound. (*Looks at LAP DANCER.*) How's it going?

HARDMAN: (*Joking.*) She'll do till summat better comes along!

LAP DANCER: (*Doesn't look up.*) Funny fucker!

HARDMAN: Shut your hole! (*Laughs, to DEALER.*) It's all good.

DEALER: I've got summat for us. (*Pulls Netto's bag from under bed.*) Check this out. (*Hands it to HARDMAN.*)

HARDMAN: (*Pulls out scanner.*) Very nice. (*Pause.*) What the fuck is it?

DEALER: It's a police scanner, innit. You can tune it in to their frequency, find out what's going on. Like, if there's a TWOC, we'll hear about it straight away. On the flipside, if we're on a job and the old bill get wind of it, we can hear it first…

LAP DANCER: (*To HARDMAN.*) Here you go.

HARDMAN: (*Drops scanner on bed.*) Nice one. (*Stands and goes to LAP DANCER, snorts a line.*) Cheers babe.

LAP DANCER: (*Sits near scanner.*) You got a toy then?

DEALER: Yeah. Where's the young 'un?

LAP DANCER: He's got her. We're gonna pick her up in a bit.

HARDMAN: (*Just snorted.*) You're gonna pick her up.

LAP DANCER: I thought you were coming?

HARDMAN: Fuck that! Gonna hang here for a bit.

LAP DANCER: But you said…

HARDMAN: Don't fucking start! (*To DEALER.*) Is this shit cut with owt? (*Rubbing nose.*)

DEALER: Probably.

HARDMAN: (*To LAP DANCER.*) You in a mood now?

LAP DANCER: No.

HARDMAN: Good. Do us a favour love, grab us a few tinnies from the shop. (*Pulls out tenner and gives it to LAP DANCER.*)

LAP DANCER: What did your last one die of?

HARDMAN: Talking back. Get a breezer for yourself.

LAP DANCER: (*Sarcastic.*) Ooh, thank you. (*Stands.*) I can't stay here long though.

HARDMAN: (*Looks blankly at her.*) Right. Stella.

LAP DANCER: Right. (*Goes to door obviously in a mood.*)

HARDMAN: (*To DEALER.*) You ever seen a woman leave a room as sexily as that?

LAP DANCER turns round and smiles at him, she exits.

HARDMAN is grinning.

DEALER: Good save!

HARDMAN: Women are easy to get round. They're fucking dumb.

DEALER: Don't be under-estimating her.

HARDMAN: What you on about? I've got her wrapped round my finger buddy.

DEALER: You do wanna be with her though, don't you?

HARDMAN: (*Nonchalant.*) Whatever. (*Pause.*) Enough of this shit. Are you ready?

DEALER: Eh?

HARDMAN: Got a little mission.

DEALER: Where?

HARDMAN: Colwyn Road.

DEALER: Who is it?

HARDMAN: You interested or what?

DEALER: (*Slight pause.*) Course I am, you know I am.

HARDMAN: Fucking old paedophile. Been scoping out a mate of mine's kids.

DEALER: What we gonna do?

HARDMAN: We're gonna give him the loud word.

DEALER: And he's definitely a nonce.

HARDMAN: I said he is, didn't I? You up for this?

DEALER: Yeah, I'm up for it.

HARDMAN: (*Pulls tyre iron out of coat and gives it to him.*) When he answers the door, you twat him. I'll push him into the house. You shut the door behind us and give me a knock if anyone comes by.

DEALER: (*Looking at tyre iron.*) Right. (*Looks at HARDMAN.*) Fucking too right!

HARDMAN: Come on then. (*Moves to door.*)

DEALER: We're going now?

HARDMAN: No, next week. Course we're going now.

DEALER: What about Jo?

HARDMAN: She'll wait. Leave the door open. Look, I thought you wanted this.

DEALER: I do.

HARDMAN: Let's do it then! (*Leaves.*)

DEALER: (*Hesitates, to self.*) Fuck me. (*Leaves.*)

Long pause, empty stage.

OLD MAN enters, singing Morecambe and Wise theme tune 'Bring me Sunshine', looks around and walks to window, looks out, gradually stops singing.

Enter LAP DANCER with drinks, she looks around, approaches window.

OLD MAN backs away from window as LAP DANCER looks out.

LAP DANCER: (*To self.*) Fucking pair of arseholes! (*Sits on bed.*) Wankers!

OLD MAN: Language.

LAP DANCER: (*Gets off bed to look for bottle-opener, finds it and opens Bacardi Breezer, drinks, sits back on bed.*) How are you George?

OLD MAN: Better than you lass.

LAP DANCER: Oh, I'm alright. Got meself in with another knobhead, nowt I can't handle. (*Drinks.*)

OLD MAN: You should be used to it by now.

LAP DANCER: I know! I should seriously consider lesbianism.

OLD MAN: (*Laughs.*) I'd probably visit you more.

LAP DANCER: (*Laughs.*) You dirty old get! (*Pause.*) Bleeding men.

OLD MAN: Sorry.

LAP DANCER: Not you. You're my guardian angel. Just, men these days.

OLD MAN: There's not as much difference between men and women as you'd like to think.

LAP DANCER: Oh aye?

OLD MAN: Aye. Well, so I reckon. These days anyhow.

LAP DANCER: Women knew their place in your day?

OLD MAN: They did, unfortunately it wasn't the right place.

LAP DANCER: (*Pause.*) Why aren't you forty years younger?

OLD MAN: And real.

LAP DANCER: Yeah, and real. (*Pause.*) Do you think I hate myself?

OLD MAN looks sad.

I think I do. Do you remember Douglas?

OLD MAN: Yes, I do.

LAP DANCER: He was lovely wasn't he? My first and last nice bloke. If I'd have let him he could've changed my life.

OLD MAN: No point dwelling on the past my love.

LAP DANCER: He had a great job and he was fit. God, he was clever. I could never bullshit him, he always knew when I was lying and rather than have a go at me he'd get me to talk. (*Drinks.*)

OLD MAN: Stop now.

LAP DANCER: 'Please don't ring me any more, I can't protect you from yourself.' That was the last thing he ever said to me.

OLD MAN: There's no need…

LAP DANCER: I'm not a mother, or a girlfriend or a human being. I'm scum. (*Drinks, long silence.*) He talks in his sleep.

OLD MAN: Who does?

LAP DANCER: Thomas. My latest flame. (*Bitter laugh.*) He talks, like a baby, in his sleep. Sounds like he's being chased by someone. 'Get off me. No please. Help me.' That's how the hard men always get me.

OLD MAN: By talking in their sleep?

LAP DANCER: No. By being little kids trapped in a man's body. All of 'em! You see this big hard exterior and believe that they'll protect you. And then you see underneath, that they're as scared of life as you are and you realise that it's you who can protect them. Look after them. But it doesn't quite work like that.

OLD MAN: Why not?

LAP DANCER: George! Don't be naïve, you've seen it for yourself. They let you in, show how vulnerable they are then they hate you for it. They hate you for seeing their weaknesses. (*Pause, angry.*) They're all fucking angry children!

OLD MAN: Maybe you should get out while you still can?

LAP DANCER: I can't George! I hate myself, I've got to keep doing it.

OLD MAN: (*Going to her.*) You are a lovely, lovely girl.

LAP DANCER: (*Backs away from him.*) I'm dirt.

OLD MAN: No you're not.

LAP DANCER: I deserve what I get.

OLD MAN: No you don't. You deserve better.

LAP DANCER: (*Very upset.*) I threw better away! (*Loud.*) I stuck with what I know and I have to face facts! I'm fucking scum!

She cries.

OLD MAN throws his arms around her, to placate and comfort.

I'm fucking scum George.

OLD MAN: SShh. Don't worry lass.

LAP DANCER: (*Soft.*) I'm scum George.

OLD MAN: Quiet now lass.

They remain in their embrace for some time.

OLD MAN breaks away to hold her face.

LAP DANCER: (*Laughs.*) Look at me! Big girl's blouse I am.

OLD MAN: No you don't young lady.

LAP DANCER: Don't what?

OLD MAN: Put them walls back up. It's high time you faced a bit of reality.

LAP DANCER: What you mean?

OLD MAN: It's time to make some choices girl. Because that's been your problem. Bad choices.

LAP DANCER: But I don't deserve any…

OLD MAN: Any better, yes I know. How about you stop making excuses for yourself? Eh? As much as you want to blame where you're from, it's you that chose certain things isn't it?

LAP DANCER: I suppose.

OLD MAN: You suppose? Forgive me Jo, because I never want to hurt your feelings, but you chose the life you're leading now. You got pregnant. You took the job. You put that filth up your nose. You chose your boyfriends. Your options might be limited, but you still have some.

LAP DANCER: I'm sorry.

OLD MAN: What you apologising for?

LAP DANCER: Being a div?

OLD MAN: Then you're apologising to the wrong person.

Door bursts open.

DEALER is having a panic attack, hyper-ventilating and shaking.

OLD MAN stands back from LAP DANCER.

LAP DANCER: What's up?

DEALER is confused and begins pacing the room.

Oi! What's up.

81

DEALER: (*Muttering.*) Don't feel good. Don't feel good.

LAP DANCER: You having one of them thingies?

She stands.

DEALER stops, looks her in the eye and nods, puts his hand to his head.

Come here.

She holds him.

HARDMAN: (*Bursting through door.*) You fucking knobhead! (*Grabs him away from LAP DANCER.*)

LAP DANCER: What you doing?

DEALER: I'm sorry.

HARDMAN: (*To LAP DANCER.*) Shut the fuck up! (*To DEALER.*) What you playing at? Eh?

LAP DANCER: (*Pushes HARDMAN away.*) Leave him alone. (*To DEALER.*) Lie down.

He does.

HARDMAN: What you bothered about him for?

LAP DANCER: (*Vicious.*) I said leave him alone.

HARDMAN: (*They square up.*) Who do you think you're talking to?

LAP DANCER: Stop being a prick!

HARDMAN: (*Tries to calm himself.*) All I wanna know is what the fuck just happened?

LAP DANCER: I don't know do I?

HARDMAN: (*Raising voice again.*) I know you fucking don't, I'm not thick. All I know is we were on a job and this loopy cunt (*Points to DEALER.*) starts babbling shite and does a runner. (*To DEALER.*) Lost your bottle did you?

LAP DANCER: (*Holds HARDMAN back.*) Get away from him and calm yourself down. (*Softer.*) I'll get him sorted, then we'll see. Won't we? Eh?

HARDMAN backs off, raising his hands.

DEALER: Cough medicine.

LAP DANCER: Where is it love?

DEALER points to cabinet.

You just stay there.

Fetches cough medicine.

DEALER: (*Is under blanket and yells out in anger.*) Fuck!

HARDMAN: (*Under breath.*) Fucking nutter.

LAP DANCER: (*Has medicine.*) Here you go.

DEALER drinks greedily from it.

Not too much.

She touches his head.

You'll be alright.

DEALER: (*Softly.*) One day, that's all I wanted.

LAP DANCER: You what love?

DEALER: (*Despairing.*) Nothing.

He lies down and faces away.

OLD MAN approaches him and whispers to him.

LAP DANCER: (*Goes to HARDMAN.*) He'll be alright in a bit.

HARDMAN: What you give him?

LAP DANCER: (*Shows bottle.*) Cough medicine.

HARDMAN: He hasn't got a fucking cough. He's got a screw loose.

LAP DANCER: Stop it. (*Pause.*) What happened?

HARDMAN: Told you. The crank started babbling and did a nash.

LAP DANCER: What were you up to?

HARDMAN: None of your business.

LAP DANCER: No, it wouldn't be would it.

HARDMAN: You been crying?

LAP DANCER: No. (*She goes to put cough medicine away.*)

HARDMAN: What did you mean?

LAP DANCER: What?

HARDMAN: (*Mimicking her.*) 'No it wouldn't be would it.' What's that mean?

LAP DANCER: It was just something to say.

HARDMAN: If you're not happy…

LAP DANCER: I am. (*Looks at OLD MAN.*) I'm happy. No problems.

HARDMAN: Good. (*To DEALER.*) No offence, but you made a right cunt of me out there.

LAP DANCER: Look, just leave him be.

HARDMAN: (*Nasty.*) Shut your mouth. (*Pause.*) Right, we're off.

DEALER: (*Sits up.*) No! You can't.

OLD MAN moves away and exits.

HARDMAN: Course I can. I'm not hanging round here watching you wig out, it's a fucking embarrassment.

DEALER: I am so sorry.

HARDMAN: You ought to be. Behaving like a fucking girl.

DEALER: I'll do better next time. You promised me you'd stay.

HARDMAN: I promised fuck all, and there ain't gonna be a next time.

DEALER: (*Stands, but is groggy.*) No. You can't go, you've got to give me another chance.

HARDMAN: Fuck off!

DEALER: (*Goes right up to HARDMAN.*) I'll be right next time I promise. I can be strong. Come on, I'm your sidekick aren't.

HARDMAN: (*In his face.*) I am not a fucking super-hero! I don't need no fucking sidekick. I don't know how you got me to fucking agree to it in the first place!

DEALER: Don't say that.

LAP DANCER: (*Pleading.*) Thomas.

HARDMAN: No! Fuck the pair of you. It needs saying. (*To DEALER.*) You are a crank. End of. You got it into your head that you can be like me, but you can't. Look at you, you're a fucking million miles from me. You can't even step outside without losing it.

DEALER stares at him.

Tell me I'm wrong. (*Pause.*) See, you know. Now I'm gonna get out of this mad-house. (*To LAP DANCER.*) You coming or what?

LAP DANCER: (*Looks at DEALER. Pause.*) Yeah I'm coming.

There's a knock at the door.

85

HARDMAN: (*To DEALER.*) Might be someone bringing your marbles back!

No one moves, another knock.

You gonna get that?

DEALER: (*Goes to spy-hole and looks through, to HARDMAN.*) Give me another chance to prove myself.

HARDMAN: Why should I?

DEALER: Charity.

HARDMAN: Fuck charity.

DEALER: I'll show you what I can do.

HARDMAN: Why would I want to watch?

DEALER: Think of it as your duty.

LAP DANCER: I thought we were going?

HARDMAN: Wait. (*To DEALER.*) My duty? (*Thinks.*) This should be worth a laugh. (*Sits on bed expectantly, to LAP DANCER.*) Come on babe.

LAP DANCER: What's going on?

Another knock at door.

(*To HARDMAN.*) What's he gonna do?

HARDMAN: No idea. Sit yourself down.

DEALER: I'm gonna answer that.

He opens door.

It's TEENAGE BOY, he is stoned.

Now then! Picked the right way in for once.

TEENAGE BOY: Can I come in?

DEALER: (*Moves to let TEENAGE BOY pass.*) I'm sound as a pound me, thanks for asking.

TEENAGE BOY: Eh?

DEALER: And have you met my good friend Bruce Wayne and his lady friend? (*Indicates HARDMAN.*) Bruce, a very loyal customer.

HARDMAN and TEENAGE BOY look at one another.

Sorry it took so long to answer the door but I was just experiencing a relatively mild panic attack. (*Grins at TEENAGE BOY.*)

TEENAGE BOY: I'll come back later, if you want?

DEALER: (*To HARDMAN.*) He likes his dope and dabbles in a little burglary does this one. Actually, I'm getting sick of the Batman reference myself. We need something original for you don't we. Something real. (*To TEENAGE BOY.*) What, in your opinion, would be a good name for a modern day super hero?

TEENAGE BOY: I wanted to talk a bit of business.

DEALER: Later. Come on, a name for a super hero.

LAP DANCER: Leave it out.

DEALER: (*To LAP DANCER.*) Humour me. (*To TEENAGE BOY.*) So, what do you think?

TEENAGE BOY: I don't know… I wanna buy that weed off you.

DEALER: First things first. We need a name for our resident super hero.

HARDMAN: This is fucking ace!

DEALER: (*To HARDMAN.*) SSSHH!

TEENAGE BOY: (*Pause.*) Erm…fuck knows. Batman?

DEALER: Oh please! You need to keep up. I thought you were bright?

HARDMAN: If he smacks you one, I won't stop him.

DEALER: (*To HARDMAN.*) Smacks me one? (*To TEENAGE BOY.*) We go way back, don't we? You wouldn't smack me one.

TEENAGE BOY: No man, you've been good to me. Always sorted me out.

DEALER: (*To HARDMAN.*) See? He's my mate, I'm his friend. (*To TEENAGE BOY.*) Something menacing, with a bit of class.

TEENAGE BOY: (*Looks slowly at HARDMAN, then to DEALER.*) Hard man.

DEALER: Hard man? (*Pause.*) I'm fucking loving that! Simple, yet accurate. Excellent that.

TEENAGE BOY: Right. (*Awkward pause.*) You've got company, can I come back later?

DEALER: (*Puts hand on his shoulder.*) Hard man! That's ace, really is. So, what can I get you this fine day sir?

TEENAGE BOY: It's alright.

DEALER: No, seriously. You mentioned that weed. What about it?

TEENAGE BOY: (*Looks nervously at HARDMAN.*) It's private, you know?

DEALER: It's not their yard is it? It's mine. Speak.

TEENAGE BOY: I wanna sell that weed on for you. (*Digs in pockets, pulls out some notes.*) I've got a deposit.

DEALER: A deposit! This ain't no fucking fridge kid. How much is there?

TEENAGE BOY: Seventy.

DEALER: (*Takes it.*) And where might you be getting seventy quid from?

LAP DANCER: (*Whispering to HARDMAN.*) Let's go.

HARDMAN: No.

DEALER: No! (*Looks at TEENAGE BOY.*) Sorry?

TEENAGE BOY: I got a mate to lend me it. (*Pause.*) I thought, seen as you won't be dealing anymore, I could shift it for you and pay you what it cost.

DEALER: There's two nine bars there. That's…eight times fifteen…one hundred and twenty…times eighteen…fuck me, my maths ain't what it used to be. But I reckon about two grand's worth on the street.

TEENAGE BOY: Yeah.

DEALER: And you wanna shift two grand's worth?

TEENAGE BOY: Yeah. I've got two ounce shifted already if I want.

DEALER: And you wanna make a down payment of seventy quid?

TEENAGE BOY: Listen, I'm good for it. Whatever it cost you, I'll give you back, plus a bit more.

DEALER: Got it sussed haven't you?

TEENAGE BOY: Yeah. (*Pulls out a polaroid camera.*) I'll give you this as well.

DEALER: What's that?

TEENAGE BOY: It's a camera.

DEALER: (*Takes it.*) It is. Let's have a butcher's. (*Examines it.*) Now this is a quality piece of equipment. And there's at least five pictures left on it.

HARDMAN: Who'd you rob it off?

DEALER: Now now Hardman, let's not jump to conclusions here. Just 'cos he presents us with a…

MARK CATLEY

TEENAGE BOY: I found it.

DEALER: There. You see. He found it.

HARDMAN: Bollox he did.

DEALER: (*To HARDMAN.*) Say cheese. (*Takes a photo of him.*)

HARDMAN: Fuck off you prick! I'll fucking smash it in!

DEALER: (*To TEENAGE BOY.*) Now then fella if you'll just shuffle over next to the happy couple, we'll get a nice souvenir of the day.

HARDMAN: (*To TEENAGE BOY.*) You take one step and I'll fucking brain you.

DEALER: Spoilsport.

HARDMAN: Get this thieving prick out of here, now!

DEALER: It's my house.

TEENAGE BOY: I ain't no thief!

HARDMAN: I said now.

DEALER: Okay. Touchy! (*To TEENAGE BOY.*) Right, this is what I'll do. You have that back. (*Gives TEENAGE BOY the money.*) And I'll keep this. (*Indicates the camera.*) And you also get. (*Goes to cupboard and takes out the weed.*)

TEENAGE BOY: (*Looks at DEALER in disbelief.*) Eh? You sure.

DEALER: Sure I'm sure.

TEENAGE BOY is just staring at the drugs.

You're gonna do well with that aren't you?

HARDMAN: What the fuck are you doing?

LAP DANCER: You can't give him that!

DEALER: Why not?

HARDMAN: Cos I don't want kids dealing!

TEENAGE BOY: Thanks man.

DEALER: (*To HARDMAN.*) See, he's happy.

HARDMAN: If you let him leave with that, I'll fucking kill you.

DEALER: Bear with me. (*To TEENAGE BOY.*) So, you're now a dealer.

TEENAGE BOY: I guess.

DEALER: You've got what you wanted.

TEENAGE BOY: Yeah. How much do you want back?

DEALER: Twelve hundred.

TEENAGE BOY: Right. No problem. It's good gear, I'll shift it.

DEALER: You got scales?

TEENAGE BOY: Yeah.

DEALER: How old are you?

TEENAGE BOY: You know how old I am.

DEALER: Tell me.

TEENAGE BOY: I'm fifteen man.

DEALER: How do you live this life at fifteen?

TEENAGE BOY: I'm not with you?

DEALER: How does a fifteen-year-old…it doesn't matter.

TEENAGE BOY: Look, cheers for this. I'm gonna get off.

DEALER: Right.

TEENAGE BOY: In a bit. (*Turns to leave.*)

DEALER: In a big bit. (*Pulls tyre iron out and strikes TEENAGE BOY.*)

LAP DANCER: No!

HARDMAN starts laughing.

TEENAGE BOY: (*Falls to floor.*) What the fuck you doing?

LAP DANCER rushes to DEALER and pushes him out of the way.

DEALER looks catatonic, drops tyre iron.

LAP DANCER: You fucking arsehole! (*To TEENAGE BOY.*) You alright?

TEENAGE BOY: (*In pain.*) Why'd he hit me?

LAP DANCER: Can you stand?

TEENAGE BOY: (*Struggles to feet.*) What have I done?

LAP DANCER: Just leave, just go. (*Bundles him out of door.*)

TEENAGE BOY: (*Confused.*) Where's my weed?

LAP DANCER: Just get out! (*Pushes him out of door, turns on DEALER.*) Of all the pathetic shite-house things I've seen…you've fucking topped it pal. You sick mother fucker…

DEALER isn't responding, LAP DANCER stops talking, long silence, HARDMAN is still laughing, to himself softly.

Fuck this.

HARDMAN: (*Laughing.*) Did you see his face? Fucking classic.

LAP DANCER: He did that to be like you.

HARDMAN: Yeah.

LAP DANCER: (*Slowly approaches HARDMAN; she takes his hands and they look into one another's eyes.*) Thomas.

HARDMAN: (*Confused.*) What's up wi' you?

LAP DANCER: Nothing. (*She kisses him on cheek, lets go of his hands and leaves.*)

HARDMAN: (*Incredulously watches her leave.*) What the fuck? (*To DEALER.*) What's all that about?

DEALER doesn't respond, long silence.

Jo!

She has gone.

HARDMAN sits on bed, long silence.

DEALER: (*Soft.*) Kill me.

HARDMAN: Kill your fucking self.

DEALER charges at HARDMAN, who stands to face him. DEALER lashes out but HARDMAN grabs him and holds him. DEALER is dementedly struggling, but eventually relents and remains in HARDMAN's grasp, passive. Eventually HARDMAN lets him go. As soon as he has, DEALER starts again. Again, HARDMAN subdues him. This time not letting him go.

(*Speaking right into DEALER's ear.*) You can't be like me. You haven't got it in you. I'm for real, it can't be faked. (*Pause.*) Face the facts kid.

He lets go.

DEALER stands motionless.

I'm out of this fucking madhouse.

He looks, disappointed, at DEALER.

DEALER: Can't stand to see yourself?

HARDMAN: What you say?

DEALER: Don't want to look in a mirror?

93

HARDMAN: You hate yourself pal, not me.

DEALER: We all hate ourselves, it's how it is.

HARDMAN: Not me.

DEALER: Yeah you do. You feel guilt.

HARDMAN: You don't know what you're talking about.

DEALER: You know you're a hypocrite.

HARDMAN: I'm not a fucking hypocrite!

DEALER: You know it! But you'll never admit it. Too tough aren't you?

HARDMAN: You've lost it pal.

DEALER: I know.

HARDMAN: I'm away. (*Turns to leave.*)

DEALER: I'm gonna kill myself.

HARDMAN: So?

DEALER: So save me.

HARDMAN: (*Pause.*) Not my problem.

HARDMAN exits.

DEALER is stood in room on his own, silent and staring at door.

DEALER: (*Soft.*) Come back. (*Goes to window, opens it and shouts out.*) Save me! (*Sits on bed, looking pitiful. Long pause.*) George? (*Pause.*) I'm sorry George. (*Pause.*) Fuck it! (*Stands.*) George! Come on, please…please. (*Pause.*) Do you want me beg? I'll beg. Got no pride anyhow. (*Goes to his knees.*) I'm pleading George. Come and get me. Come on. Talk to me. (*Nearly in tears.*) I don't want to be like this. (*Long silence.*) Fuck you then you old cunt! You're not real anyway! It was me who knew about Feng

94

Huang not you. It was me who lost me mam, not you. (*Stands.*) Fuck the lot of you! (*Pause.*) And fuck me. (*Goes under bed and pulls out bottle of gin and sleeping tablets.*)

(*To audience.*) Hello again. I said I'd talk to you at the end and it is the end… Of me. I don't want you to feel sorry, or sad. This is my decision, I made it some time ago and it is what I want. You don't have to watch if you don't want. (*Lifts out a carrier bag, removes a bottle of gin and some tablets.*) The Last Supper. Jesus had twelve mates with him at his, I have no mates, just customers, so I will be dining alone this evening. (*Takes some tablets and washes them down with gin.*) Do you know what the biggest killer of young men is in this country? Aged about twenty to thirty-five? Cancer? Road accidents? Heart disease? None of the above, our top answer is…suicide. As we gloriously gallop into our twenty-first century on this earth the biggest killer of men, in their prime, is suicide. Themselves. Six thousand a year. That can't be fair, can it? What sort of world is this? Is it just some sick fucking joke? Here you go, here's a life, now this should be filled with experience, joyous moments. Hardship cosmically balanced with beauty. Beauty! Don't make me look out of that window again. Beauty is obsolete, it's been erased. (*Drinks and takes more pills.*) I'm twenty-eight years old and I've had enough. I don't want to wake up any more. Life has passed me by (*Drinks.*) but it's okay, I got someone to tape it! (*Laughs, softly. Angrier.*) And what is my legacy? Huh? What do I leave? (*More pills and booze.*) A big round fuck all! A pure ball of nothing. (*More animated, approaching the edge of stage.*) You know what? I'm fucking happier now. I know it's not gonna happen any more. I'm gonna be free of this shit. And if I meet the devil, I'm gonna shake his hand, sell him an eighth and pull up a chair. (*Drink and pills.*) And if baby Jesus happens to greet me I'm gonna stamp on him. Be nice to everyone and it'll be cushty? Piss-taking bastard! (*Sits and drinks, slowing down, talks dejectedly.*) Who am I kidding? It's no-one's fault but me own. (*More pills.*) There's no point in talking. It's all been said before. Don't feel sad for me. (*Takes more pills, sits silently, is drowsy now.*) Don't look at me. I'm a fraud. (*Finishes the pills, takes out a roll of masking tape and tapes his hands so he can't use the phone.*) I don't wanna be changing my mind and phoning someone. (*Drinks awkwardly like he is wearing mittens. Yawns.*) Fucking hell, anyone'd think I'd just taken a shit load of sleeping pills! (*Pause.*) I often thought…I…fuck it! Doesn't matter what I often thought. (*Drinks. Tries to throw a pill in the air and catch it in his mouth, he is giggling.*) I forgot to write a note. (*Stands, unsteadily, finds a pen, but can't pick it up, looks up, as if to God.*) Give a man a break you fucking cunt! (*Walks back to bottle and pills but falls suddenly.*) Whoa! Shit. (*Crawls to bottle, pulls over the bag of weed and uses it as a pillow, long silence, DEALER is weeping.*) I don't feel well. (*We can hear his crying, he lies still. Slowly he tries to raise his hands to his mouth to bite off the masking tape, fails.*) Mam.

Long pause.

Door is kicked open.

Enter HARDMAN, dressed more dramatically in long leather coat and gloves. He has a scarf around his lower face. He looks very dark. He moves purposefully. He approaches DEALER's prone body and takes his pulse. He picks up DEALER in his arms and stands still.

DEALER: (*Very drowsily opens his eyes.*) Thank you.

HARDMAN exits, with DEALER in his arms.

The End.